The power of Babel

Teaching and learning in multilingual classrooms

Viv Edwards

Trentham Books in association with the Reading and
Language Information Centre, University of Reading

First published in 1998 by Trentham Books Limited in association
with the Reading and Language Information Centre

Trentham Books Limited
Westview House
734 London Road
Oakhill
Stoke-on-Trent
Staffordshire
England ST4 5NP

Reading and Language
  Information Centre
The University of Reading
Bulmershe Court
Earley
Reading RG6 1HY

Designed and typeset by Text Matters

Printed in Malaysia

British Cataloguing in Publication Data

A catalogue record for this book is available from the British Library

ISBN: 1 85856 095 0

The power of Babel

Teaching and learning in multilingual classrooms

1

3

Contents

Foreword

It is common these days to hear policy-makers and school administrators talk of the school as a 'learning institution'. In doing so they usually imply not only that schools are institutions where pupils are engaged in learning, but also that the school itself must continue to learn from its own collective experiences if it is to adapt to the challenges of the 21st century.

Unfortunately, one of the most significant challenges faced by schools, namely the increasing cultural and linguistic diversity of school populations, is frequently ignored in policy debates. Issues related to diversity get submerged in the rhetoric of accountability, raising standards, and improving literacy. As a consequence, it is hardly surprising that misconceptions about bilingual pupils continue to abound. For example, pupils are often assumed to have overcome the 'language barrier' when they have acquired the ability to converse relatively fluently in English. We know, in fact, that it can take much longer for pupils to bridge the gap in academic aspects of English. Similarly, pupils' first languages are still frequently seen as either irrelevant to their academic progress or even as detrimental to attainment.

This volume, so aptly named *The Power of Babel*, dispels these and other myths in the most effective way possible: actual classroom practice is documented that starts from the premise that other languages and cultures are resources to be developed and sources of enlightenment and enrichment for both pupils and teachers.

For example, when pupils carry out language surveys of their classroom, school or even community, they realize that they can become generators of new knowledge rather than just consumers of information. When the school learns from pupils and community members how to welcome parents and new pupils in their own languages, the notion of 'the school as a learning institution' begins to take on real significance. When multilingual word processing enables ethnolinguistic communities and pupils to express the funds of knowledge they possess, the school is truly preparing pupils to thrive in a global community characterised by rapid cultural and technological change.

This inspiring and unpretentious book illustrates vividly how we can implement a global education philosophy together with a multicultural and anti-racist perspective. By implication, the volume also suggests that pupils who graduate from school with a monocultural perspective are ill-prepared to contribute to their society. They are simply not educated for a national and international reality characterised by unprecedented diversity of culture, language, 'race' and sexual orientation. It is clear that educators must also be attuned to these changing realities if they are to prepare their pupils for the world of the 21st century. This volume points us in the right direction. It offers no formulas but it does promise us the excitement of learning along with pupils how to create new interpersonal spaces in classrooms where our own and our pupils' intellectual, cultural, and personal identities can be affirmed.

Jim Cummins

Acknowledgements

The power of Babel grew directly from the courses for mainstream teachers in Berkshire and Oxfordshire run jointly by the University of Reading and Berkshire Equality Services. Urmi Chana, Anna Chapman, Ann Whittle, Sharon Flemming, Jagiro Goodwin and myself were involved in planning, and Rowland Eno, Prue Goodwin, Karen Jarman, Sarah Mitchell, Kiran Oram, Janet Page, Chris Routh and Judith Scott helped us deliver the courses. My thanks go to all those who helped to make 'Meeting the needs of bilingual pupils' such a valuable learning experience for all concerned, but most especially to Urmi Chana and Ann Whittle for their imagination, humour and unstinting support.

Thanks equally to the Berkshire and Oxfordshire teachers who took part in the courses and the children and colleagues in their schools who cooperated with them on their projects. Their efforts were marked by enthusiasm, a genuine spirit of enquiry and a great excitement at the outcomes. Ultimately, the choice of case studies used to illustrate this book was fairly arbitrary – for every one included, another three could have been used to make a similar point.

Thanks also to the plethora of insightful practitioners and researchers to whose work I allude in the course of this book, and, in particular, to Chris Dickinson, Jagiro Goodwin, Eve Gregory and Angela Wellings; and to Dafydd Morriss for the illustrations and Bert Weltens for the Dutch translation on page 52.

Last but by no means least, thanks to those who kindly read and commented on earlier drafts of this book: Urmi Chana, Elizabeth Coehlo, Hetty Edwards, Angela Redfern and Ann Whittle. As ever, the final responsibility for any errors or omissions remains with me.

The title of this book has been 'borrowed' from a publication of the same name produced by PRAESA (Project for the Study of Alternative Education in South Africa). I am grateful to Carole Bloch for drawing attention to its powerful symbolism and to the similarities in aims between PRAESA and the teachers whose work is reported in the pages which follow.

Viv Edwards

1 Introduction

Classrooms where children come from two or three or ten or more different language communities are an established feature of schools in many countries. Teachers working in these schools are keen to ensure that all children achieve their potential. The depressing truth, however, is that many children from ethnic minority communities continue to underperform (Gillborn & Gipps, 1996; National Center for Educational Statistics, 1994). Limited proficiency in English is often invoked to explain disappointing levels of achievement.

The correlation between English language skills and educational achievement is, of course, only partial. Some bilingual communities fare much better than others: children from China and Japan, for instance, tend to enjoy far greater academic success than African-American and African-Caribbean children.

Various explanations have been offered for these different patterns of performance. Writers such as Ogbu (1992) make a distinction between voluntary and involuntary minorities. Voluntary minorities move to the new country to seek better economic prospects or greater political freedom and tend to do much better in school than involuntary minorities, like the descendants of African slaves or aboriginal populations in North America and Australia. Involuntary minorities often assume an identity which questions or opposes the values of the dominant group as a way of maintaining their self-worth; differences in language and culture become more rigid than is the case in voluntary minorities, offering a possible explanation for different patterns of educational achievement.

Teacher expectations would also appear to play an important role. In Japan, children from the low class Burakumin community tend to do very poorly in school. When transferred to the USA, however, they are simply perceived as Japanese, and perform on the same high level as their compatriots (Ogbu, 1992).

Economic factors, too, have been shown to have a strong relationship with educational achievement. Recent years have seen marked increases in levels of poverty in many parts of the developed world and corresponding disparities in expenditure on education among different local authorities and school districts (Taylor & Piché, 1991). Against this background, it is not altogether surprising that the rhetoric of equality of educational opportunity has not been translated into equality of educational outcome.

Attempts to explain patterns of underperformance purely in terms of limited proficiency in English are thus very unsatisfactory. This does not, of course, detract from the fact that children need to learn English as rapidly and efficiently as possible. Second language learners are aiming at a moving target: their learning must proceed more rapidly than that of native speakers if they are ever to catch up. A 'common sense' view has prevailed for many years that children's first languages have no part to play in this process. *The power of Babel* sets out to challenge this myth by exploring the potential of linguistic diversity as a tool for learning.

Bilingualism or not?

The presence of bilingual children in schools throughout the English-speaking world is by no means a recent phenomenon. Almost every society is in fact a multilingual society; the only parameters which vary are the extent and tolerance of diversity. It is noteworthy, for instance, that governments through space and time have sought to control ethnic minorities through language. The notorious review of education in Wales contained in the 1847 'Blue Books' decries the use of Welsh on the grounds that it 'dissevers the people from intercourse which would greatly advance their civilisation, and bars access of improving knowledge to their minds'. One hundred and forty years later, the same sentiment can be detected in *English, our English,* a pamphlet produced by John Marenbon, one-time chair of the Schools Examination and Assessment Council:

May politicians and committees keep strong in their common sense, distrustful of experts and chaste towards fashion. May God grant them sharpness of mind and firmness of resolve, for in the future of our language lies the future of our nation.

Nor is this an exclusively British phenomenon. Earlier this century, Theodore Roosevelt dismissed the linguistic heritage of immigrants to the USA, insisting on the supremacy of English and the imperative that the crucible should produce 'Americans of American nationality' and not 'dwellers in a polyglot boarding house'. Similarly negative views were expounded as recently as 1995 by Newt Gingrich who, according to *The Los Angeles Times* of 4 August, believes that bilingual education 'slows down and confuses people in their pursuit of new ways of thinking'.

The old debate took some new twists with the arrival of large numbers of non-English-speaking children in Britain in the 1950s and 1960s, and in Canada and Australia after the lifting of the discriminatory immigration policies which operated well into the 1960s. At first, traditional views of bilingualism seemed impervious to change, in spite of obvious inconsistencies. When associated with powerful elites – from the Latin-speaking intellectuals of yesteryear to English-speaking children in French immersion programmes in Canada today – bilingualism is a highly prized skill. In contrast, the bilingualism of powerless minorities – Bangladeshi children in East London, or Somalis in Toronto – is totally undervalued. For many years, research offered a veneer of respectability to the prejudices of the wider society, underlining the inferior educational performance of bilingual children, while overlooking

social class differences and comparing the achievements of monolinguals with bilinguals operating in their weaker language (Baker, 1996; Cummins, 1996).

Several developments made it possible to challenge conventional wisdom. The political activity of various groups from the 1960s onwards – the Welsh Language Movement, the Parti Québecois in Canada, the ETA movement in the Basque country – placed language issues very firmly on the map. Political developments have been mirrored by developments within socio- and psycholinguistics. Jim Cummins (1996), for instance, has been particularly influential in providing alternative models of how bilinguals learn. The metaphor of the brain as a receptacle with a finite capacity – so that bilinguals would never be able to speak either of their languages as well as monolinguals – has been replaced with the metaphor of a dual iceberg. In this view, the surface features of a speaker's languages are represented by two peaks appearing above the water. Below the water, however, is a common underlying proficiency which makes it possible to transfer cognitive skills from one language to another. The logical conclusion is that maintenance of the first language will help – not hinder – children's acquisition of a second language.

A great deal of recent research supports this notion (see, for instance, Ramirez, 1992; Beykont, 1994; Verhoeven, 1994; Thomas & Collier, 1997). The findings of Wayne Thomas and Virginia Collier (1997) deserve particular attention, partly because of the very large number of children who form the basis for their study and partly because they have tracked these children over many years. When comparing the effects of various kinds of intervention on children entering school with no English at the age of five, they found little evidence of different patterns of performance in the first three years of school. Gradually over the next four years, however, some unmistakable trends emerge.

The children who consistently performed best – in fact, above the level of average monolingual English speakers – were those attending two way bilingual programmes where approximately equal amounts of time are spent studying each language in classes with children from both the English-speaking and minority language communities. The poorest performances are associated with the traditional 'pull-out' model, where children are taught the sounds and structures of English in 'withdrawal classes' for second language learners. Ironically, the children with the least exposure to English are those who ultimately perform best, thus providing convincing backing for the notion of the interdependence of languages and the transfer of skills. There is no evidence to support the 'common sense' idea that teaching efforts should focus exclusively on English to the detriment of development in the first language.

Linguistic incorporation

Bilingual education is not an unusual phenomenon: it exists in many different forms in the vast majority of countries in the world (Baker, 1996). It tends, however, to be very much a minority concern. In Canada, the main initiatives are focused on the French immersion programmes. Heritage language teaching is provided on parental demand, but takes place most frequently outside the regular school day. In the UK, bilingual education is limited to Welsh schools in Wales (Edwards, 1991), Gaelic in Scotland (MacKinnon, 1991) and European schools

(Baetens-Beardsmore, 1994). Even in the USA, which probably has the greatest diversity of bilingual programmes, most language learners are taught in mainstream classrooms where English is the exclusive medium of instruction.

Bilingual education is, of course, a viable proposition only in situations where there are significant numbers of speakers of the same language and, very often, schools include small numbers of speakers of many different languages. It is important to remember, however, that the English-only classroom is not the sole viable alternative to bilingual education. American researchers such as Beykont (1994), Campos & Keatinge (1988), Ramirez (1992) and Lucas & Katz (1994) all argue that the extent to which children's language and culture is incorporated into the curriculum is a significant predictor of academic success.

It is not difficult to see why this should be the case. We have already considered the cognitive and intellectual benefits associated with bilingualism. The links between language and identity provide another compelling reason for incorporating diversity. It is often argued that one of the most unfortunate consequences of colonialism is the attempt to convince the colonized that the stigma attached to them, their language and their culture is deserved. The tendency to ignore or trivialize minority languages in school has very damaging effects (Wong Fillmore, 1991). Children may shift to English, possibly creating communication difficulties with parents, grandparents and other family members; in the process they are made to feel ashamed of who they are. Reactions such as these are hardly conducive to the feelings of comfort and confidence which go hand in hand with successful learning.

In contrast, by encouraging the use of community languages, teachers are sending powerful messages about the value which they attach to other languages to all the children in the class; they are also enhancing the status of bilingual children. Monolingual children, for their part, are able to increase their knowledge of and sensitivity towards other languages and cultures.

Even in the absence of bilingual education, aspects of children's prior knowledge can be used to activate their learning. When discussing poetry, for instance, it is possible to draw on children's previous experiences – irrespective of the language in which they were enacted. What kinds of themes do poets usually explore? Do the same themes recur across cultures? What forms do poems take – from the Japanese haiku to the Islamic calligraph?

For children who have experience of school in the home country, the use of other languages in spoken and in written form can also serve as a valuable bridge to the acquisition of English. Access to bilingual support in the form of human resources, dictionaries and dual language books can make the task of language learning far more efficient. A brief explanation in the child's dominant language can remove frustration and eliminate misunderstanding at a stroke. And by creating opportunities for using other languages in activities alongside English speakers – writers' workshops, dialogue journals, taking notes, etc – the focus is on what beginner bilinguals can do, rather than on what they cannot.

By refusing to treat second language learners as blank slates and by constantly seeking ways of drawing on their prior knowledge, learning is made more relevant for bilingual children and much richer for their monolingual peers. *The power of Babel* has grown directly from mainstream teachers' efforts to activate existing knowledge.

The context for this book

The introduction of a national curriculum in England and Wales 1988 brought a radical shift in educational policy. For the first time, children as young as five years old were required to study a range of 'foundation' subjects in addition to the 'core' subjects of English, mathematics and science. Many competent primary teachers were very anxious at the thought of having to work on science topics which they had never fully understood, handling databases in Information

Technology when they were not sure how to boot up the system, or recalling distant memories of key differences between the Tudors and the Stuarts. At the same time they were required to familiarize themselves with 'national curriculum speak' – attainment targets, key stages, programmes of study – and devise and apply complex, unfamiliar and very time-consuming recording and assessment procedures. Curriculum documents were published, proved unworkable and revised at headlong speed.

All professional development in the years following the Education Reform Act 1988 inevitably focused on the implementation of the national curriculum. Teachers were in effect given permission to sweep matters relating to the needs of bilingual pupils under the carpet. It was against this background that the Department for Education (DfE) announced a new professional development initiative in 1995. Bids were invited from higher education and local education authority (LEA) partnerships for courses which would prepare mainstream class and subject teachers to 'meet the needs of bilingual pupils'. This was a highly significant development at the end of a protracted period in which bilingual learners had almost disappeared from the official educational agenda.

At the same time, radical educational reform was extending to a review of the criteria for the Section 11 funding which had underwritten most of the support offered to bilingual pupils. The requirement that LEAs submit proposals for specific fixed term projects had the desired effect of making spending on bilingual pupils more accountable. However, it also narrowed the uses to which Section 11 monies could be put. The exclusive emphasis was now on English language teaching, making it very difficult, for instance, to continue the professional development role which had traditionally been undertaken by language support services or to promote community language teaching initiatives. The introduction of the Single Regeneration Budget in some authorities (Passmore, 1994) also had the effect of putting language support in competition with other services, such as housing and community services. Further unfortunate by-products of the reforms were the loss of many posts, the threat to job security and the undermining of morale.

Pressure from teacher organizations produced a gradual softening on the part of the DfE, including the announcement of the 'Meeting the needs of bilingual pupils' initiative. Questions have been raised about whether this initiative was too little, too late and scepticism expressed over whether the real aim was to remove the need for specialist support teachers, thereby reducing costs. None the less, the flurry of activity which followed in its wake was highly significant. For the first time in seven years, bilingual pupils had resumed their rightful place on the educational agenda.

Initiatives in Berkshire and Oxfordshire

The University of Reading collaborated with Berkshire Equality Services and Oxfordshire Section 11 Language and Curriculum Project to provide in-service training for almost two hundred teachers over a two year period. A central feature of the ten day courses was a research project which required teachers to apply what they had learned to their own classrooms. The issues explored in this book reflect many of the topics covered in the course and draw extensively on teachers' classroom projects. Some of these teachers work in schools where a very high proportion of the children come from minority communities; others work in schools where there are very few children who speak English as an additional language.

Case studies based on course members' projects are supplemented from time to time with accounts from other innovative practitioners. While most accounts are based on primary schools, a small number address children in secondary schools; many of the primary case studies could be easily adapted to a secondary context.

A note on terminology

While *The power of Babel* examines initiatives in British classrooms, the issues which it raises will be familiar to teachers in many parts of the world. The terminology used to discuss linguistic diversity, however, varies from one setting to another and from time to time. In writing for an international readership, it is important to explore areas of potential confusion at the outset.

It has proved very difficult, for instance, to find a satisfactory umbrella term for children with varying levels of proficiency in English. 'Speakers of English as a second language' is a cumbersome label, sometimes abbreviated to ESL or E2L, which lacks precision: English is indeed a second language for many children, but for some it is a third or even fourth language. 'English as an additional language' or EAL is a more accurate description, which is currently gaining in currency, at least in the UK. British educators balk at the American use of 'limited English proficiency' or LEP, arguing that this term stresses what students lack – fluency in English – rather than their ability to speak at least one other language. 'Bilingual pupils' has thus emerged as the preferred terminology in the UK, despite the fact that it may seem singularly inappropriate in discussing children who arrive in school speaking no English. The assumption here, of course, is not that we are dealing with 'balanced bilinguals' who speak two (or more) languages with equal levels of proficiency, but with children in various stages of acquiring a second or additional language.

Terms for the languages which children bring with them to school are equally problematic. 'first languages', 'home languages' and 'mother tongues' are all in common usage; they are accurate in some cases, but not in others. Many Pakistani children, for instance, say that they speak Urdu, the language of high culture which they learn in special classes, when the language of the home is actually a closely related dialect of Panjabi. Following the handover of Hong Kong, growing numbers of Cantonese-speaking children are attending classes in Putonghua, the national language of the People's Republic of China. Many third and fourth generation Polish children are taught the language of their grandparents in community run classes, but speak only English at home. It would be inappropriate to describe Urdu or Putonghua or Polish as the first language, the home language or the mother tongue of the children in question. The use of 'community languages' in Australia and the UK and 'heritage languages' in Canada and the USA conveniently sidesteps these issues. A community or heritage language may or may not be the first or home language or the mother tongue of the children in question.

This introduction began with the assertion that children need to learn English as rapidly and efficiently as possible if they are to compete on equal terms in a predominantly English-speaking country. The focus on linguistic diversity in the pages that follow is wholly compatible with this goal.

2 Finding out

Second language learners are sometimes treated as though they were a homogeneous group. Nothing could be further from the truth. The personal histories of children who arrive in school with little or no English are many and varied.

Place of birth

The first important distinction is where children were born. Children born abroad will have to make adjustments to life in the new country. Their linguistic situation may also be very different: British born children, for instance, include Welsh speakers and third and fourth generation Italian speakers whose parents are striving to keep alive a heritage language in the home in the confidence that English will be acquired through exposure to the wider society. In contrast, children born abroad will have varying levels of fluency and literacy in English.

Language background

Language background can also give important clues about children's previous experiences. However, it can be dangerous to make broad generalizations. Chinese children may have come from Hong Kong, Taiwan, Malaysia or the People's Republic of China. The financial situation of families from the so-called tiger economies is likely to be much stronger than those from the People's Republic; their exposure to English is also likely to have been much greater. There are also differences in religion between speakers of the same language: Panjabi speakers include Muslims, Sikhs and Hindus; Bosnians include Orthodox Christians, Catholics and Muslims. Children from countries where education is universal and free are more likely to be highly literate. No such assumptions can be made about the levels of literacy in families from countries where access to formal schooling is more difficult.

Reasons for migration

Some families make the new country their permanent home; others spend a few years abroad before returning home. Some come for economic reasons, others as political refugees. Their situations are clearly very different.

An understanding of the special case of refugee children is particularly important (Rutter 1994; Rutter & Jones, 1997; Coelho, 1998). While migration is a stressful experience for all children, the trauma of the refugee experience may complicate the process of adjustment. Most will have witnessed death and violence and many will have lost or been separated from family and friends. Many will have been exposed to continuing violence and great hardship in refugee camps. Further uncertainty will have met them on arrival in the new country where they may have changed addresses several times and attended a number of schools in a short space of time.

Under such circumstances, it is not surprising that children often exhibit one of two classic responses: the first is highly disruptive behaviour, the second is withdrawal. Expertise in meeting the needs of refugee children is gradually increasing. Counselling is sometimes available, particularly in areas close to airports. Efforts are also being made to inform teachers better about the needs of refugees.

My name's Ayaan mohmed Ali I am 13 years old
I come from Soomaali I was Born in mogdisho
I Have 12 sisters and brothers I Have mother and
father But adon't ol is day and Late Because
Soomaaliya is faytin I don't lake my self
Beacouse I havent mother and father
efriday I Thought My famili.
I like To ✗ school Becouse I want learnng inglish

Ayaan's moving account of her family in Somalia

Responsibilities of teachers

The challenge for teachers, then, is to find out as much as possible about the children they are working with. A child who has recently experienced the trauma of civil war in Bosnia will have very different needs from one whose father has a temporary placement in a Japanese company abroad. Children who can already read and write in their first language require different kinds of support from those who have little or no previous experience of literacy.

Information gathering on the language and culture of children represented in the school is clearly very important for central aspects of school life, such as admissions procedures and assessment. It also has implications for the curriculum. Children can be actively involved in exploring different languages or naming systems, for instance, as part of language study, an essential element of the national curriculum for English.

In this part of the book we look at different kinds of information which teachers require in meeting the needs of bilingual pupils and at the different approaches to collecting and sharing this information. In particular, we focus on:

- surveys which establish the range of languages spoken
- directories which bring together information on the different language groups represented in the school
- information on different names and naming systems, essential both for accurate record keeping and for showing respect
- school admissions information,
- assessment issues in English and children's first languages.

The richness of dialects and other languages can make an important contribution to pupils' knowledge and understanding of standard English. Where appropriate, pupils should be encouraged to make use of their understanding and skills in other languages when learning English.

English in the national curriculum (DfE and Welsh Office, 1995: 2)

Language surveys

A consistent finding of language surveys is that children speak many more languages than was previously thought. This observation applies both to schools where there is one large minority group – and where teachers assume that this is the only language spoken other than English – and to schools where there are only very small numbers of bilingual children. As Nicholas (1994) points out, language surveys firmly place the question of diversity on the educational agenda and can be a very useful catalyst for change.

Because many children are also fluent English speakers, it is often assumed that they are monolingual. But even when they are not proficient speakers, questions about the languages used in the home by parents and grandparents often reveal at least a passive knowledge of other languages. Language surveys increase awareness of the extent of diversity in the school.

Surveys also have the effect of raising the profile of other languages. They enhance the status of bilingual children and give them the opportunity to demonstrate their skills. At the same time, they broaden monolingual English-speaking children's horizons and increase their awareness of language.

Planning a survey

Language surveys can, of course, be planned and carried out by teachers as a largely administrative exercise. However, it is possible to transform the process by involving children. Surveys offer valuable experience of devising questionnaires and collecting and analyzing data. Children can also help to design and produce displays of the findings. Most important,

making children an integral part of the project gives them a real sense of belonging to a multilingual community.

Collecting data from the whole school can be an ambitious undertaking. One way forward is to start with your own class. Displays and presentations of findings in assembly may well inspire colleagues to undertake a similar survey in their own class.

Children sometimes report that they speak Indian or Pakistani or African, or that they don't know which language they speak. In both cases, the most likely explanation is uncertainty about the questioner's motives. Even very young bilingual children are usually able to label their languages.

The school needs to work hard to show respect for other languages and cultures. Otherwise children may conclude that teachers are either hostile or indifferent. When they hide the fact that they know other languages or claim to speak 'Indian' or 'African', this is a sure sign that the school has not succeeded in demonstrating a commitment to diversity. Before embarking on a language survey, teachers need to make clear to children their own positive feelings about other languages and cultures and the achievements of bilingual pupils, for instance, in ways suggested in the case studies which follow.

Further reading

- *The other languages* by Viv Edwards (RALIC, 1996; PETA, 1997) which contains a photocopiable language survey form.
- *Language diversity surveys as agents of change* by Joe Nicholas (Multilingual Matters, 1994).

CASE STUDY: DISCOVERING DIVERSITY

An important first step in promoting diversity is to establish just how many languages are spoken in the school, something which works best when children are active partners in the process. Lynne Hutchings describes how she set about this task with a group of Year 4 children in Larkrise First School, Oxford.

The seven of us talked about the languages that we used in different situations. Some of the children said they had learned languages when they were on holiday. Nabeel and Marina both speak Urdu at Mosque and Panjabi and English at home. Sravya speaks Hindi, Telegu and English. Speaking two languages appears to be a highly desirable skill: Tanya was adamant she spoke French and Welsh, while Oisin insisted that he spoke Irish. After discussion we decided that, for the purpose of the survey, speaking another language would mean being able to hold a conversation in that language, something which neither Tanya nor Oisin could do in their 'second languages'.

I handed each of the children a copy of a survey that had been carried out in another school to give them ideas for the kind of questions they might like to ask. They found this survey too long and one of them asked if he could stop half way through. They decided their survey would have to be very short, particularly if they were going to cover around 300 children in the school. Each child then wrote down the questions which they felt should be included. These included 'Which country were you born in?' and 'Which religion do you follow?' After some discussion we decided that, although these were interesting questions, they had little to do with which languages people speak every day. The children finally voted for the following questions:

- Which languages do you speak?
- Do you know quite a lot of that language?
- Which country does that language come from?
- Which language do you speak at home?
- Which language do you speak the most?

Each pair of children chose a class and took a list of names to make sure that no one was missed out. We had decided that the researchers would ask the questions because some of the younger children might not be able to read the questionnaire.

When all the information had been collected, the children were able to create graphs. We could clearly see the spread of languages, especially on the bar chart. We discovered that fifteen different languages were spoken and that most teachers were unaware of the diversity outside their own classrooms. All the staff would like to know more about the languages and cultures represented in the school and were enthusiastic about my intentions to create a language directory.

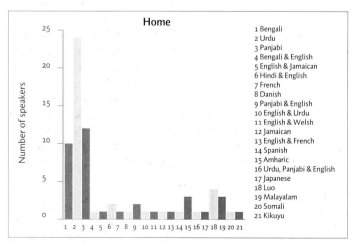

The languages spoken at Larkrise First School

Language directories

Once teachers have established the range of languages spoken in the school, it is a natural development to want to find out more about the languages in question and the people who speak them. Compiling a language directory is the logical next step.

Languages

Accurate information on linguistic background is essential. A new arrival from Sierra Leone was recently placed in lower streams on admission to secondary school because it was assumed that he spoke no English. This decision is, of course, highly questionable: limited proficiency in English cannot be equated with intelligence. However, it is even more unsatisfactory when we take into account that English is the official language of Sierra Leone and that the boy had previously attended an English medium school.

Conversely, teachers sometimes assume that children speak English when this is not the case. Newcomers from St Lucia and Dominica, for instance, may speak a French creole when they arrive from the Caribbean, while children from other Caribbean islands may speak a variety known as Patwa or Creole which differs systematically from standard English (Coelho 1988; Dalphinis, 1991). Many children born in the new country will continue to codeswitch between the local variety of English and the distinctively Caribbean variety which serves as a marker of their identity (Edwards, 1986).

Notions of which languages are spoken in other countries, or the range of different countries where particular languages are used can be very hazy. For instance, there is often confusion over the differences between Serbian and Croatian, or Urdu and Panjabi. By the same token, many people are not aware that, although Tamil came originally from India, there are large communities of Tamil speakers in Singapore, Malaysia and Fiji.

Linguistic information can also be fascinating. Does the language in question use tone to distinguish between words, as is the case in Chinese and Yoruba? Does it use a system of grammatical forms – or honorifics – to show respect for the interlocutor? Does it exist in written form or is it a purely spoken language?

Culture and religion

Directories provide an excellent opportunity to record information on the languages spoken by children in your school. But they can also be used to gather other information which will help build up a clearer picture of children's previous experiences. For instance, Gujarati-speaking families who have arrived via East Africa usually enjoyed a more affluent lifestyle than those who came direct from India. There are other differences within the Gujarati community, too. The mainly Hindu population is divided into different castes which influence the choice of marriage partner. The smaller Muslim groups include a range of different sects, from the conservative Isthna Asaris to the liberal Ismailis.

Literacy

Other kinds of information are also very helpful. It is likely, for instance, that recently arrived children from countries like Japan and Korea where literacy rates are high will be able to transfer existing skills to the task of learning to read and write English more easily than Somali children whose education has been disrupted by civil war.

A basic knowledge of the writing system that children have experienced is useful. Does the writing go from left to right, from right to left or from top to bottom? Do the marks on the page represent meanings as in the case of Chinese characters, syllables as in many Indian writing systems, consonants as in Arabic and Urdu, or vowels and consonants as in alphabetic writing? Does the writing hang from the line as in Panjabi and Bengali or rest on the line as in English? Or are the words formed within an imaginary square as in Chinese? (see p. 74).

Names

Information on names can also be usefully included in language directories. (see p.16).

Potential pitfalls

Teachers embarking on language directories sometimes produce vast tomes which represent a valuable summary of their own voyage of discovery but are unlikely to whet the appetite of busy colleagues. It is important not to lose sight of the ultimate goal – an accessible, user-friendly document.

Data collection can be a long and tedious process, so it is always a good idea to involve as many colleagues as possible. It is a good idea to look first at what is already available and to adapt it to your needs.

Ideally the language directory will form part of any information packs offered to new members of staff. It should be treated as a working document, which can be extended to reflect changes in the population of the school as they happen.

Sources of information

Encyclopedias and the internet are both useful sources of information when compiling a language directory. Reference works of particular interest include:

- *Concise compendium of the world's languages* by George Campbell (Routledge, 1997)
- *Handbook of scripts and alphabets* by George Campbell (Routledge, 1997)
- *Languages of the world* by Kenneth Katzner (Routledge, 1994).
- *The atlas of world languages* edited by Bernard Comrie, Stephen Matthews and Maria Polensky (Bloomsbury, 1996)
- *The other languages* by Viv Edwards (British version, RALIC, 1996; Australian version, PETA 1997).

Most parents are delighted to offer help to teachers working on directories. They are able to explain how names function in their culture – a question which most reference works overlook. They are also able to comment on the accuracy of information you have collected.

CASE STUDY: MAKING A 'LANGUAGES BOOK'

Children whose bilingualism has previously been ignored often feel confused by sudden attempts to promote linguistic diversity in school. Notice how in this account the teacher prepares the ground with several activities which establish her positive feelings towards bilingualism.

Twenty seven of the four hundred children attending Whiteknights Primary School in Reading speak a total of thirteen different languages among them. The fact that bilingual pupils formed a small proportion of the school community and that all but one were fluent in English meant that linguistic diversity had remained a largely hidden resource.

Against this background, Lorraine Beskin set out to explore the cultures and heritages represented in the school. She started by designing a language survey which invited colleagues to list the names of children who spoke, read or wrote other languages outside school and to specify the languages in question.

An audit of school resources revealed just three books in other languages. Lorraine decided to redress this imbalance by collecting dual texts and story tapes from the library service which reflected the range of languages spoken in the school. The children were given time to look through the selection and most recognised at least one other language. They were clearly excited by the number of languages which they were able to identify as a group.

Two tasks were set for the bilingual children, who were visibly gaining in confidence. The first was to make 'Welcome' signs for the classroom doors in English and their own language. These signs served as a reminder of the diversity of cultures in each class and colleagues commented on their surprise at the number of different languages.

The second task was to jointly produce a 'Languages book' containing information on the children and the countries they came from. The children worked on this in school and at home, with parents either checking spellings or, in some cases, providing the translations. The finished product was shared throughout the junior classes before being placed in the entrance hall for other children and visitors to read.

The project achieved many different ends. It allowed bilingual children to assume the role of experts. It gave their parents a chance to become more actively involved in their learning. It raised awareness among both staff and children of the cultural and linguistic heritages represented in the school. Hopefully, it will also send important messages to any new bilingual pupils about the value which the school attaches to bilingualism and the fact that other children have gone through similar experiences.

Willkommen in unserer Klasse

Ich bin Samantha Gellert, zehn Jahre alt. Ich komme aus München (Deutschland) und habe fünf Jahre in Florenz (Italien) gelebt. Seit November 1995 bin ich in England. Ich spreche deutsch, italienisch und englisch. Ich freue mich, in England zu sein.

Welcome in our class

J am Samantha, ten years old. J come from Munich (Germany) and have lived in Florence (Jtaly) for five years. J have been in England since November 1995. J speak German, Jtalian and English. J am happy to be in England.

Benvenuto nella mia classe

Jo sono Samantha, ho dieci anni. Vengo da Monaco (Germania) ed ho vissuto à Firenze (Jtalia) per cinque anni. Sono in Jnghilterra da Novembre 1995. Parlo tedesco, italiano e inglese. Sono contenta di essere in Jnghilterra.

A page from Whiteknights School's 'Languages Book'

Names

Names are very much part of who we are. When people call us by the wrong name, it can be embarrassing. When people mispronounce our names, it can be irritating. Occasionally, other children and even teachers make fun of children's names in a way which is tantamount to bullying. The teacher who consistently and deliberately called Satwinder 'Sidewinder' added insult to injury by insisting that Sidewinder didn't mind at all.

Some names, of course, are very difficult for English speakers. For instance, Urmi and Tahir pose less difficulty for Irish and Scots speakers who pronounce 'r' in all positions in words, than for speakers of many other English dialects. Other names, such as Fakir, Shital and Asma can be problematic because they have unfortunate associations for English speakers. These difficulties aside, most names can be pronounced with reasonable accuracy and a minimum of effort.

Different systems

Naming systems are often very complex and differ to an astonishing degree from one culture to the next (Edwards, 1996). In Japan, for instance, family names come first. In Pakistan, the pattern for boys' names is different from the pattern for girls. It is important to use both names of Chinese children: Mei Ling, not Mei or Ling. Mothers and fathers do not necessarily share a family name.

While teachers can't be expected to understand the intricacies of every naming system, they do have a responsibility for getting children's names right. The simplest way of dealing with this question is by asking parents at admission interviews what they want their child to be called and what they wish to be called themselves (see School admissions, pp. 18–19).

Children's own preferences

Children deal with the question of names in many different ways. Some feel unhappy when their names are mispronounced and are confident enough to insist that teachers and children get it right. Some are anxious about being seen as different and prefer to Anglicize their names. Many Chinese Christian children have both a Chinese and an English name and choose to use their English name in school. African-Caribbean children are also sometimes known by different names at home and in school. It is important to establish children's preferences and respect their wishes.

CASE STUDY: A ROSE BY ANY OTHER NAME?

The correct pronunciation of names is an issue which affects many children. Girls called Cheryl, for instance, may want to be called Sheryl, not Cheryl. Boys with Welsh names such as Dafydd [Davith] object to being called Dafid. Pat Choules set out to investigate this question with Year 6 children at the William Penn School in Slough.

Pat considers herself to have a very poor ear for languages and suspected that she and many of her colleagues were mispronouncing children's names. Her class designed a questionnaire eliciting information on what children were called by their parents, friends and teachers. Two children were given responsibility for collecting the data.

Twenty out of seventy Year 6 children reported that teachers pronounced their names differently from parents and friends. Common mistakes included placing the stress on the wrong syllable, eg Mubash'ir for Mub'ashir and using the wrong vowel, eg Atif for Ateef. Various tales emerged in the course of the project. Yogesh's name had been pronounced correctly as Yo'gesh for three years

before a new teacher began to call him 'Yogesh and other children in the class quickly followed the teacher's example.

Interesting patterns emerged:

- Some children were unhappy about the ways their names were pronounced. The teacher listened carefully to how they said their names and devised her own transcription system.
- Some children felt uncomfortable about 'authentic' pronunciations and were happy with an Anglicized version which didn't depart too radically from the original.
- A small number of children preferred an English nickname.

An important conclusion was that Year 6 – just before transfer to secondary school – was not the best place to start considering the pronunciation of children's names. A more practical approach might be for teachers to ask children to pronounce their names at the beginning of each year and to make their own transliterations. These could then be adjusted, if necessary, in consultation with the children.

School admissions

The ideal opportunity both for finding out about the family and for communicating essential information is when children first start at the school.

Interpreters

It is important that in their first encounter with the school, parents and children should feel as comfortable as possible. Sometimes parents who lack confidence in English bring a more fluent relative or friend. On other occasions, it may be possible for a bilingual member of staff to act as interpreter. Alternatively, it may be necessary to arrange a follow-up interview with an interpreter from the translation and interpreting services provided by many local education authorities and school boards.

The admissions form

Time spent thinking carefully about what to include on the admissions form will reap ample rewards. Although the form should not be unduly long or cumbersome, make sure that detailed information is collected on both names and language use.

Names

Given the differences in naming systems, it would be naive to assume that children and parents will share the same family name, or even that children's personal names come first (see p. 16). Ask parents for the following information:

- the full name of the child
- the full name of both parents (if appropriate).

Then ask:
- what they wish the child to be called
- what they wish to be called themselves.

Adopt a standard convention for recording this information. For instance, the child's preferred name can be underlined – Mohammed <u>Arif</u> Akram – and the form of address for parents can be added in brackets after their full names – Fazeelath Begum (Mrs Akram).

Languages

Schools are required to complete returns on the different languages spoken by the children. However, it is very useful to build up a more detailed picture of family language use than is required for official statistics. This information serves a number of purposes. It helps teachers understand children's previous experience of language and adjust their communication strategies accordingly. Where the child can be admitted to one of several classes, it influences decisions as to the most appropriate class. For instance, if the child is a Farsi speaker, and there is only one other Farsi speaker in the year group, it would make sense to place them in the same class. Finally, building up a fuller picture gives the school a chance to express a positive interest in the language(s) of the home.

Parental involvement

Recording parents' willingness to help in school on the admissions form achieves two ends: it makes it clear that parental involvement is welcomed and it provides another opportunity for demonstrating the school's commitment to diversity.

It is helpful to provide examples of the kind of involvement which would be welcome, as shown in the form for parents on p.19.

Many parents help out in school on a regular basis. Can you tick the box next to any activities where you would be able to help:

☐ art and design
☐ chess
☐ cooking
☐ music
☐ reading
☐ reading or telling stories in other languages
☐ school trips
☐ writers' workshop
☐ writing in other languages

A form inviting parents to participate in a range of school activities

Effective liaison

The information collected on the admissions form is of little value if it is simply filed away. However, when stored on a database, information can be retrieved on children's languages and religion, parents' ability to read and write other languages or willingness to help, all of which will be invaluable in planning cross-curricular activities. It is also important that information of this kind should be made available in an easily accessible form when children move from class to class, or school to school.

Keeping track

In areas where there is rapid population movement, it is important to collect information on country of birth, parents' country of birth and date of arrival. This makes it possible to keep track of demographic changes in a school or across the system and to track the progress of specific groups of students.

CASE STUDY: PUTTING THE RECORD STRAIGHT

Lorraine Beaven, a nursery teacher at Ryvers School, was convinced of the value of information on children's home backgrounds in planning more effectively for teaching and learning, but she was unsure about how this information should be collected and presented to her colleagues.

She finally decided on two forms. The first (see p.20) recorded full information on each child; the second (see p.21) was a summary of information on all bilingual children in the class, which could be kept for ready reference in the register and used in planning across the curriculum.

Using the data on her own class, she was able to identify parents to help the class learn a nursery rhyme in Panjabi and to translate a class book into Panjabi, Gujarati, Hindi and Arabic. The interest generated has also resulted in a number of new offers of help from parents for storytelling and other activities.

Name to be known by	Country of origin	Religion	Language 1	Spoken Written Read (circle)	Language 2	Spoken Written Read (circle)	Language 3	Spoken Written Read (circle)	Dietary needs	Clubs, community schools, religious centres, hobbies or any other information, etc
				S W R		S W R		S W R		
				S W R		S W R		S W R		
				S W R		S W R		S W R		
				S W R		S W R		S W R		
				S W R		S W R		S W R		
				S W R		S W R		S W R		
				S W R		S W R		S W R		
				S W R		S W R		S W R		

Class record

Ryvers Combined School: Pupil home background

Full name:	Date of arrival in UK:
Name to be known by:	Festivals celebrated:
	Siblings 1:
Date of birth:	Dietary needs:
	Siblings 2:
Father's name:	Religion:
	Siblings 3:
Mother's name:	Place of birth:
	Siblings 4:

Details and dates of long absences abroad:

Details of clubs, community language schools, religious centres, hobbies and sports clubs:

Previous schools

Name and type of schools:	Town or country:	Dates – from/to

Languages – *Spoken Written Read (circle)*

S W R

S W R

S W R

Use of languages in the home: *Spoken Written Read (circle)*

	Pupil	Father	Mother	Adult	Adult	Child	Child	Child	Child
	S W R	S W R	S W R	S W R	S W R	S W R	S W R	S W R	S W R
Language 1									
Language 2	S W R	S W R	S W R	S W R	S W R	S W R	S W R	S W R	S W R
Language 3	S W R	S W R	S W R	S W R	S W R	S W R	S W R	S W R	S W R

Individual record

Assessment

Assessment is important for establishing a baseline against which future progress can be measured. Equally important, it can be used to plan individual work programmes to move children's learning forward. However, the assessment of second language learners is extremely problematic.

Standardized tests

The first area of difficulty concerns the standardized tests which are widely used in schools. Sometimes these tests draw on knowledge which is assumed to be general but which is actually specific to a particular group: British children will know that the Victorian era ended in the early years of the twentieth century; American children will know that Thanksgiving is held on the last Thursday in November and Canadian children that this holiday is in the middle of October. It cannot be assumed that children from outside the geographical area concerned will have access to 'general knowledge' of this kind. Yet many standardized tests draw on culturally embedded information.

Cultural bias also intrudes in nonverbal tests. For instance, because problem solving is seen in many societies as a collaborative activity, decontextualized tests which require individuals to work in isolation may seem very strange. Whatever the nature of the test, standardization is likely to have taken place on a monolingual English-speaking population very different from the multilingual communities found in many schools. Standardized tests are inevitably poor indicators of children's actual potential. They often give no information about what tasks – or range of tasks – a child can perform and therefore offer little guidance on what the teacher needs to do to move them on.

First language assessment

An assessment of proficiency in the home language is important for several reasons:

- *A full picture* If assessment is confined to children's performance in English, the picture which emerges will be unsatisfactory. Information on whether a child can understand or speak or read and write (an)other language(s) is important both in planning cross-curricular activities and in showing respect for linguistic and cultural diversity.

- *Children who speak no English* Although some tests exist in languages other than English, this is another area fraught with difficulty. A test devised for Muslim speakers of Mirpuri Panjabi, for example, might contain items which were culturally and linguistically challenging for Hindu Panjabi speakers from Harayana. In any case, testing in other languages is a matter of purely academic interest for the very large number of languages where no suitable assessment tool exists.

- *Bilingual children with special needs* It is often very difficult to decide with any degree of confidence whether problems experienced by bilingual children should be attributed to their language development or to specific learning difficulties. Teachers often argue with good reason that undue anxiety about bilingual children's language development is misplaced and that, providing they find themselves in a stimulating and supportive learning environment, they will catch up. In most cases this approach is well-founded. Occasionally, however, specific learning difficulties are over-looked and, as a result, bilingual children receive additional support much later than their monolingual peers.

- *Consultation with parents* In all cases, consultation with parents or guardi-ans is essential. They are best placed to provide the fullest picture of children's previous and ongoing experiences. They are also likely to be acutely aware of any problems: it is important to establish, for instance, how the devel-opment of the child in question compares with that of siblings.

Bilingual colleagues can provide valuable information on second language learn-ers. An informal conversation can often establish whether the first language is at an appropriate level for children of their age. They can also sometimes uncover worries which are having an adverse effect on children's well-being and progress.

Further reading

- *Assessing the needs of bilingual pupils* by Derryn Hall (David Fulton, 1995)
- *Assessment in the multi-ethnic primary classroom* edited by Pat Keel (Trentham, 1994)
- *Bilingualism and special education* by Jim Cummins (Multilingual Matters, 1984)

3 The welcoming school

Many teachers respond to descriptions of successful initiatives to promote diversity in the classroom with protestations of, 'That would never work in our school!' or, 'Our parents would never do that!' Often they choose to counter success stories with tales of unfortunate experiences of their own.

There is usually a pattern when things go wrong. Although expectations of the roles of parents and teachers vary a great deal from one culture to another, most failures can be explained in terms of a breakdown in communication rather than a lack of parental interest. When teachers set out to welcome families and understand the barriers which stand in the way of more active participation, the response is very different from when they wring their hands and place the blame on parents.

A developmental process seems to operate in most schools. First, teachers need to inform themselves of the nature and extent of linguistic and cultural diversity in the student population; next, positive steps need to be taken to acknowledge this diversity. Only when teachers have thought carefully about how parents perceive the school can they hope to encourage greater participation.

Tokenism

Teachers have become very aware of the dangers of tokenism: sometimes characterized as the 3S approach (saree, samosa and steel band) in the UK and as the 3F (food, festivals and famous men) approach in Canada. If the school commitment to diversity does not go beyond an Indian dance group or welcome posters on classroom doors, it is certainly a matter of concern. Attempts to ensure equity for all children need to move beyond the token to address 'institutional racism' – those aspects of school organization or teacher expectations which disadvantage children from minority communities. Examples of institutional racism might include the expectation that black children will be good at sport but not at academic subjects; the placement of children in a low ability group on the basis of their current level in English rather than their actual potential; or the exclusion of other languages and cultures from the curriculum. Looking at ways of making the school more welcoming is an essential precursor to addressing questions of institutional racism.

In this part of the book, we look at two approaches to making schools more welcoming to parents and children:

- the visual environment: is the world portrayed in posters and displays and home corners exclusively Anglo and Eurocentric, or does it accurately reflect the wider society?
- home-school communication and attempts to involve parents in their children's learning in school.

First impressions

When children, parents and visitors enter the school, first impressions are very important. Schools are print rich environments, full of signs, notice boards, books, displays of children's work and even messages on T-shirts. But is this print in English only or are other languages and scripts on display? And do the people and clothes and customs shown in books and posters reflect the range of people represented in the school?

We should never underestimate the impact of 'the hidden curriculum'. When teachers take steps to reflect the diversity of the wider community in school, the response can be dramatic: the little boy who, on seeing Panjabi on the computer in his nursery, called out in disbelief, 'Look, that's my language on the screen!'; children who had claimed they spoke only English but who now enthusiastically demonstrated writing in another script; the boy listening to a dual language tape, who sprang to his feet with a cry of: 'That's Urdu!'

Nor should we minimize the impact of the hidden curriculum on the community outside. Teachers often complain that it is difficult to persuade parents from minority communities to come to parents' evenings or social events, or to act as classroom helpers. Few understand the overpowering sense of strangeness which many parents experience on entering the school. Attempts to reflect other cultures in the visual environment help reduce feelings of 'not belonging'.

Entrance displays

Particular importance is often attached to the appearance of the school's entrance. Welcome posters in other languages, a parents' notice board, and photographs of members of staff all send the message that school is a friendly place which welcomes parents and children and values diversity.

Signs, labels and nameplates

Most schools are big enough to be disorientating for newcomers and many use signs to help visitors find their way around. Trays and coat hooks are marked with children's names. Labels are used liberally in classrooms and the library.

Reasonably priced signs in many different languages are available from a number of sources listed in the *AIMER Yearbook*. Alternatively, home-made signs and labels can be wordprocessed or handwritten with the help of parents and bilingual colleagues.

One of a range of multilingual notices for schools produced by Barnet Education Support and Training

Welcome notice available from Collins Educational

Toys and games

Do all the dolls in nursery and reception classes have white faces? And if the selection includes black dolls, are their features European or African? Do cooking utensils in the home corner reflect the range of cultures represented in the wider society? What kind of clothes are in the dressing up box? Do children have access to crayons representing a range of skin colours?

A growing number of companies now supply toys and games from many different cultures. Commercial items can be usefully supplemented with donations from home, such as shalwar kameez and other items of clothing, and food packets for the class shop.

The *AIMER Yearbook* (see p.78) includes resource lists for *games, sports and toys, music* and *arts and crafts*.

Artefacts and musical instruments

Teachers' and parents' own travels will often generate artefacts which can be used in displays. Music is also a useful source of cultural diversity. Do children have the chance to listen to music and experiment with instruments from outside the European tradition?

Printed matter

In addition to a range of books in other languages (see, for instance, pp. 59–61), newspapers, magazines, cards and calendars provided by parents and colleagues make useful additions to classroom resources.

CASE STUDY: MAKING AN ENTRANCE

Imogen Badnell of Slough Centre Nursery School works on the principle that a school entrance is like a shop window, giving a taste of what lies inside. She believes that it needs to be welcoming and to create a sense of a safe and caring atmosphere. As a new member of staff, she was keen to make contact with parents and felt that a useful way forward would be to produce a display linking home and school.

I felt that a world map would make a vivid centre piece and excite interest. I talked to the headteacher about my ideas and booked time in the next meeting to discuss it with the rest of the staff. In the meantime I composed a letter to parents explaining what we hoped to do and asking for their help. A mother and a colleague translated the letter into Urdu and Panjabi.

I was very pleased with the initial enthusiastic response from parents. I found that many were willing to help but needed reassurance

that what they had in mind would be acceptable.

In making the display, it was difficult to decide which of the photographs I should use. They included pictures of different homes and vegetation in Jamaica, farm animals, a city mosque, a mother in her nurse's uniform in Pakistan, as well as family and friends. I kept the ones showing the nursery children or close relatives to put around the map and placed the others in an album. These photographs served as a starting point for discussions about how other people live, the different clothes that people wear and the diversity of their customs and climates. Samples of different scripts provided by the parents were also added to the display, which rapidly became a talking point with parents and children.

We were all amazed at the diversity of our children's backgrounds, information which has been very useful not only in understanding the make-up of the nursery but also in making choices for rejuvenating the library.

CASE STUDY: DISPLAYING DIVERSITY

Mary-Ann Brooks of Lea Infant School in Slough was concerned about the visual environment of the school. Although the staff were very conscious of the different cultural backgrounds represented in the school and provided a range of multilingual notices and information for children and parents, she felt this awareness was not always reflected in the images around the building.

After reading and consulting widely, she decided on a set of criteria:

- material should represent a range of cultures with non-stereotypical images
- representatives of different cultures should form a central part of the action and not appear as token, background figures
- images should be accurate, not caricatures
- all displays should show respect for different ways of life.

With these criteria in place, she set out to do an audit of the school's display materials. She found a wide variety of posters and religious artefacts and a selection of Asian drapes. However, she rapidly became aware that some of the posters didn't meet the new criteria and

that there were many important gaps. There were, for instance, no images of people from minority communities doing 'western' jobs, or paintings by non-European artists.

Having completed the audit, she began to look for suitable new resources. Using information from the AIMER database, she visited specialist bookshops and sent for catalogues from suppliers of multicultural posters and artefacts.

Realizing the importance of involving colleagues in the project, she asked the various year groups what they felt should be included in display materials and what they required for the next term. Armed with this information, she approached the headteacher and together they agreed a rolling programme of renewal whereby as much as possible of the material would be acquired over the coming year. They also discussed sources such as museums, tourist information offices and embassies which would loan materials or provide them free of charge, and the possibility of taking photographs of children in the school.

Home-school communication

A visual environment which acknowledges the diversity of the wider society is an essential first step in establishing good relations between home and school. However, a range of other steps can help create a welcoming atmosphere.

Home visits

Most schools arrange for some kind of introduction for new parents and children. This may take the form of visits to the classroom in the term before the child starts school or an information session for new parents. In many schools, nursery and reception teachers also undertake home visits. Although these visits can be very time-consuming, the benefits are enormous.

Home visits are an important bridge for children starting school. When they enter their new classroom they find someone who has met younger brothers and sisters or other members of the family and has seen them in the more relaxed surroundings of the home. Teachers and children are able to draw on this shared experience.

Home visits also have benefits for parents. Meeting teachers on their own territory often transforms relations between home and school. When parents and teachers are able to chat informally about children and get to know each other on a personal level, foundations are laid for an open and trusting relationship. It is very much easier for a parent who has had personal contact of this kind to approach teachers when problems arise. In the same way, teachers have a better understanding of the family situation and much greater confidence in involving the family more fully in their children's education.

Visits to families with limited English work better when the teacher is accompanied by an interpreter – a bilingual colleague or community outreach worker. However, visits can be valuable even in the absence of an interpreter. Teachers sometimes confess to feelings of paralysis at the thought of 'talking' to parents with little or no English. The reality of home visits is almost always very different. The warmth of hospitality offered and received creates a bond which makes future contact more comfortable.

Class books with photos of staff and children as well as classroom activities and routines form a useful focus for home visits, irrespective of parents' competence in English. Sharing a book or playing a game can also be a useful first step in forging a relationship with the child. Even better, leave a book for the child to return on the first day of school.

Open classrooms

Many schools have an open classroom policy where, instead of saying goodbye to children at the school entrance or the classroom door, parents are welcome to come into the classroom at the start and finish of the day to admire their child's efforts. Opportunities of this kind allow parents to have a better idea of what actually takes place in school, to exchange information with the teacher and also to establish good relations.

Access to the headteacher

It is very important that parents should have easy access to the headteacher. In many schools, the head or deputy makes sure that they are available to greet parents and children in the morning and to say goodbye in the afternoon. In this way, many minor issues can be dealt with promptly and informally. If the head-teacher also ensures that the first half hour of the day is not timetabled, more serious problems can be dealt with as they arise. Rapid access of this kind will help reduce anxiety and prevent crises becoming dramas.

Parents' evenings

Parents' evenings are generally considered a very important channel of communication between home and school. Complaints from teachers about the poor attendance of ethnic minority parents are common. Experience has shown, however, that when arrangements are examined carefully, it is possible to achieve a very high rate of attendance, even in schools which have a disappointing record:

- *Timing* Parents often fail to attend for practical reasons. Are interviews held only on one evening? By offering two different options – afternoon appointments immediately after school on one day, and evening appointments starting at 6 pm on another, parents who work shifts will find it much easier to attend.
- *Interpretation* Are interpreters present for parents' evenings and, if so, are parents informed that this will be the case?
- *Communication* Are parents informed of meetings by letter and, if so, are these translated? In schools with high proportions of bilingual pupils, announcements in the ethnic minority press (see illustration) are sometimes very successful, particularly in the case of middle and secondary schools where teachers don't come into daily contact with parents. In nursery and infant classes, parents can be given a

personal invitation by the teacher when they collect their children in addition to a letter of invitation.

Slough and Eton C.E. School

Ragstone Road, Slough SL1 2PU Tel : (0753) 520824

Headmaster : H. S. Pattar

For pupils starting Secondary School in September 1995

Open Evening
Wednesday 19th October
7.00 p.m. - 9.00 p.m.

ਇਸ ਸਕੂਲ ਦਾ ਮੁੱਖ ਨਿਸ਼ਾਨਾ ਪ੍ਰਮੁੱਖ ਡਿਸਿਪਲੀਨ ਤੇ ਵਿਵੇਕ ਵਿਦਿਆਕ ਮਿਆਰ ਕਾਇਮ ਕਰਨਾ ਹੈ। ਇਸ ਤੋਂ ਪਹਿਲਾਂ ਤੁਸੀਂ ਆਪਣੇ ਬੱਚਿਆਂ ਲਈ ਸਕੂਲ ਚੁਣੋ, ਕਿਰਪਾ ਕਰਕੇ ਤੁਸੀਂ ਇਸ ਸਕੂਲ ਆਉ।

ਓਪਨ ਈਵਨਿੰਗ
ਬੁਧਵਾਰ ਸ਼ਾਮ 7 ਤੋਂ 9 ਵਜੇ ਤੱਕ 19 ਅਕਤੂਬਰ 1994

1993 ਵਿੱਚ ਪਾਕਿਸਤਾਨ ਦੇ ਮਸ਼ਹੂਰ ਕ੍ਰਿਕਟ ਖਿਡਾਰੀ ਇਮਰਾਨ ਖਾਨ ਅਤੇ 1994 ਵਿੱਚ ਬਰਤਾਨੀਆਂ ਦੇ ਸਿੱਖ ਜੱਜ ਸ੍ਰੀ ਮੋਤਾ ਸਿੰਘ ਜੀ ਨੇ ਸਕੂਲ ਵਿੱਚ ਆਕੇ ਸਭ ਮਾਨ ਵਧਾਇਆ।

ہمارے اسکول کا مقصد ہے کہ اعلیٰ تعلیم اور اچھا نظم و ضبط قائم کرنا ہے اس سے پہلے کہ آپ اپنے بچوں کے لئے اسکول کا چناؤ کریں ہمارے اسکول تشریف لائیں

أوپن ایوننگ

بدھ 19 اکتوبر 1994ء کو 7 بجے سے نو بجے شام

اعزاز: اس اسکول کو یہ اعزاز حاصل ہے کہ 1993 میں عمران خان اور 1994 میں برطانیہ کے جج موتا سنگھ نے اس اسکول دورہ کیا

Parents and pupils in Middle Schools are warmly welcomed to visit us on this evening.
The Headmaster and Staff are committed to :

* High standards of achievement for all boys and girls.

* Maintaining excellent standards of behaviour and discipline.

* Giving parents clear information to support the progress of every pupil.

Come and meet the staff and see our facilities on 19th October. You will be given a guided tour of the school and full prospectus.

The Headmaster's speech in the Main Hall is at : 8.00 p.m.

A map showing the location of the school is overleaf.

An announcement for a parents' evening in a local minority newspaper.

Social events

Another common complaint is that parents from ethnic minority communities rarely attend social events organized by the school. If this is the case, it is important for schools to look closely at the nature of the events on offer. Wine and cheese evenings, for instance, are unlikely to be acceptable to many Muslims. In contrast, international evenings tend to be universally popular.

However, a note of caution should be sounded about international evenings. If the school's commitment to diversity starts and ends with opportunities for food tasting and performances of song and dance, then cries of 'Tokenism!' are valid. International events only play a useful role in the context of a wider commitment to diversity.

It would also be a mistake to think that all events must be inclusive. Women who, for cultural and linguistic reasons, feel uncomfortable in many of the social events offered by the school may none the less welcome attempts to organize meetings where they can gather to chat informally among themselves or hear about aspects of school life through an interpreter.

Written communication

In many schools, all written communication – newsletters, school documents, permission letters – takes place in English. Various arguments are offered in support of this practice. For instance, when many different languages are spoken in a school, it is often felt impractical to arrange for translation. However, very often there are only one or two main language groups within a school. In practice, speakers of languages with few representatives in the school are well aware of the organizational and resource implications of translation and raise no objections if their own language is not included.

Another common position is that translation is unnecessary because many parents are illiterate in the community language. Sometimes this is indeed the case. However, the fact that many other parents can read and write the community language would seem a powerful argument against this stance.

Alternatively, it is sometimes suggested that, because many parents speak and read English, translation is inappropriate. This stance fails to take into consideration the wider implications of the decision to make documents available in other languages. One obvious aim of translation is to ensure efficient communication; another is to make a statement about the importance – and status – which the school attaches to bilingualism.

Practical considerations

When a school decides to translate some or all of its written communication with parents, certain practical issues need to be considered. The first is: who translates? It is important to remember that translation requires considerable skill. Sometimes bilinguals lack the necessary skills and confidence but feel pressured to comply. Translation can also be a time-consuming process – if bilingual colleagues are to serve in this role, they need to be given time during the working day. Parents may be prepared to help, but they should never be pressurized. Alternatively, many LEAs and school boards offer translation services.

In all cases, translation must be scheduled. One way forward is to send all communications home on the same day each week, thus ensuring an agreed deadline for any items to be included, and the translator can allocate time accordingly. Since parents will be looking out for letters, this course of action will also have the effect of greatly increasing the efficiency of 'pupil post'.

Transliterations of other scripts into the roman alphabet can also be usefully considered. Parents are happy to model pronunciation and will sometimes be

var taro alvar aavo te ka, aavo te ka

Bridegroom, why is your best man like this, why like this?

This transliteration of part of a Gujarati wedding song allows the English speaker to approximate to what has been written in Gujarati; it can also be useful for children who speak Gujarati but are not able to read the script

When the English-speaking teacher asked a colleague to 'write' some geography vocabulary 'in Panjabi', the colleague provided a transliteration of the English in Gurmukhi script as in (a) below and not a translation as in (b) below:

a ਮਾਉਂਨਟੇਨ pronounced as mountain

b ਪਹਾੜ pronounced as pahar (the Panjabi word for 'mountain'

'Write "mountain" in Panjabi'

able to offer a 'romanized' transliteration. Parents and children are happy to make allowances for English accents.

A note of caution: when parents and other bilinguals are asked to write something in another language, they sometimes respond by providing a transliteration of the English into the other language script rather than a translation. It is important to explain very clearly what you require.

The case studies which follow illustrate the practicalities of establishing a close working relationship between parents and teachers. One focuses on the efforts of teachers to make it possible for new parents to support each other and their children's learning. The other logs a teacher's progress in involving parents in many different aspects of work in her class.

CASE STUDY: THE 'NEW TO OXFORD' GROUP

Cuttleslowe First School in Oxford is typical of many schools which serve not only a very mixed local community but also a large transient population of – in this case – university students. Staff at the school were very aware that the Parent-Teacher Association and the school governing body were dominated by white middle class parents and were anxious to involve a wider cross-section of the school community. They set about this task through their 'New to Oxford' parent group. The group had previously met sporadically, but lacked focus.

When Heather Varden convened the first gathering of the year, the 18 parents attending decided that meetings would be held on the first Thursday of the month, and would alternate between purely social gatherings and meetings with a specific focus. They also decided on a class representative scheme – every class would have a named parent who would liaise with newcomers. Again at parents' request, permission was sought to use one of the large boards in the foyer for notices about the group's activities.

Together teachers and parents generated a wide range of ideas for ways in which parents could support their children's learning:

- *Making tapes* It was agreed that children should have access to their home language while at school and several parents volunteered to make tapes in their own languages. Details of how this should be done would be decided at a future meeting.

- *Storytelling* A few of the parents were already involved in joint storytelling sessions with a teacher, the parent reading or telling the story in their home language. This idea attracted additional support.

- *Festivals* Parents undertook to inform the school of any festival which was important for their child so that teachers could plan for work in class and school assemblies, as appropriate.
- *Fundraising* Some parents were keen to raise money by providing items for an international food stall at the school fete and sports day. It was agreed the money would be used for buying multicultural resources for use in home corners.
- *Writing in other languages* Parents agreed to bring in items such as calendars, newspapers and cards written in other languages which could be used in home corners and displays. Several parents also volunteered to make labels in their own languages for displays.
- *Topic boxes* A long term aim is to collect items to make resource boxes on themes such as homes, food and clothes.

- *Resources for parents* A small library has been started to help answer parents' – and teachers' – questions about children's bilingual development.

Useful books and resources

- *A parents' and teachers' guide to bilingualism* by Colin Baker (Multilingual Matters, 1995)
- *Being bilingual* by Safder Alladina (Trentham, 1995).
- *Bilingual Family Newsletter* available from Multilingual Matters, Frankfurt Lodge, Clevedon Hall, Victoria Road, Clevedon BS21 7HH.

Festival calendars are available from:

- NES Arnold, Ludlow Hill Road, West Bridgford, Nottingham NG2 6HD
- The Festival Shop, 56 Poplar Road, King's Heath, Birmingham B14 7AG.

CASE STUDY: PARENTS IN THE CLASSROOM – A TEACHER'S JOURNAL

Sue Budden charts the progress of attempts to involve parents more fully in her class of mainly Indian and Pakistani children at Montem County First School in Slough. The positive response of the children to her attempts to promote linguistic diversity is very much a feature of the journal. So, too, is the importance which she attaches to empowering parents.

23 January I taught the children *Head, shoulders, knees and toes* in Panjabi today to try and raise the profile of their language in the classroom. They really enjoyed it and told me words for other parts of the body that they knew. Later we were tasting breads and the children told me names of some of the Indian breads in their languages.

I approached several parents to ask for their help in writing nursery rhymes in Panjabi / Urdu and for sitting with us when we have our sharing sessions. I have had some positive responses. Mrs Guhataour doesn't write Panjabi but her husband does, so she is trying to

get him to come into school. Mrs Ali would like to come and write out some nursery rhymes in Urdu. Mrs Afzal seemed quite shy and unsure of herself, but she would like to come in at our sharing times. I will see Mrs Baig and Mrs Chaudry tomorrow.

25 January Today I asked Mrs Chaudry if she would like to come and tell stories in her own language and she was thrilled to have been asked. The children asked if we could sing *Head, shoulders, knees and toes* in Panjabi again today. Afterwards some of the English-speaking children asked if we could sing it again in English and one boy even wanted us to sing it in French.

26 January Today at sharing time I encouraged those children who could to use a language other than English. Some of them preferred to do this with a friend rather than the whole class. I told them that Mrs Afzal would be coming in the next day and that she would be able to understand and talk to them in their home language.

Mrs Baig came in today to write nursery rhymes in Urdu. She enjoyed this and even wanted to take it home to finish. Some of the children went over to have a better look and asked her questions about what she was doing.

28 January Mr Guhataour is going to come into school next Tuesday morning to do some Panjabi writing alongside the children. One little girl decided that she wanted to do her Writers' Workshop in Panjabi today. At the end of the lesson she read her story out first in Panjabi, then in English.

31 January This afternoon Mrs Chaudry came into the classroom and told the children the story of 'The hare and the tortoise'. She explained what a hare and a tortoise were beforehand and how each of them move. She then read the story in Urdu explaining as she went along any parts she thought they might not understand. At the end she asked the children questions about the story in Urdu and they answered in Urdu.

I talked to her about the idea of using pictures that can be stuck on a board while the story is being told. She thought this was a good idea and would like to try it next week. I will work with her initially, then she would like to do it by herself.

2 February Mr Guhataour came in today and sat with two children. They were going to write a story together in Panjabi but in the end they wrote about being good and drew a picture to go with it. Mr Guhataour also wrote out a nursery rhyme in Panjabi to go in our book while the two children were doing their writing. He was quite shy but said he would like to come in again.

4 February The children now like to answer the register in their own language as well as in French and English, so we have different languages on different days.

This afternoon Mrs Baig came in to continue writing out the nursery rhymes in Urdu and again the children showed interest in what she was doing. I can make her writing into a book now.

We had a sharing session today and the children are much more confident about using their languages. The monolingual children are also enthusiastic about listening to them.

7 February I saw Mrs Chaudry today and gave her a story with the cut-out figures so she can practise at home for Monday. I won't be there but she is still keen to come in.

The children have now started greeting me in the morning in Urdu and Panjabi and they try to teach me new words to say.

8 February Mrs Ali came in today and started working with a group of three children. They had the story of *The very hungry caterpillar* which they retold in Urdu using the pictures I have made. They then told the story again, this time recording it. At the end of the day the class sat in a horseshoe and the three children who had recorded the story stood at the front. I played the tape and held the book, with the three children telling me when to turn the pages. Other children in the class laid the accompanying pictures in the middle of the horseshoe in the correct sequence. It worked very well.

10 February The children still like to answer in their own language but now they like me to use the appropriate language in reply so they are teaching me the necessary words. One of the monolingual English-speaking children is fascinated with other languages and likes to answer in Urdu.

14 February Today I have organized a workshop day. I have approached and enlisted several parents who will come in tomorrow to work with the children and me telling stories in Urdu and Panjabi, making up story packs and making booklets about colours, numbers and weather. We will also try to complete the illustrations for the nursery rhyme book.

15 February Workshop day. Some of the parents couldn't come in the end and the ones who were there could only write Urdu. So the Urdu books are finished and the Panjabi ones still have to be made. In the morning before the parents came, I had groups of children illustrating the nursery rhyme books. Then Mrs Pervez came in and wrote Urdu in some books about colours, numbers and weather. She couldn't remember some of the weather words so we looked them up in a bilingual dictionary. The children then illustrated them. Afterwards she sat with a group of children retelling the story of *Little Red Riding Hood* and recorded them.

This afternoon Mrs Ali wrote some signs in Urdu for me. She then sat with a group telling the story of *Gail's birthday* which we had recorded in English on Monday. At the end of the afternoon Mrs Baig came in and told a story to a small group of children. She then recorded the nursery rhymes from the book we had made in Urdu and wrote the title on the cover. Another parent who hadn't been able to come to the workshop said she wanted to take the nursery rhyme book home so she could produce a Panjabi version. The children really seemed to enjoy the day; so did the parents.

16 February Mrs Bahia brought the translation back to school and we now have a Panjabi version of the nursery rhyme book. I feel I have learned a great deal this half term and am looking forward to continuing after the holiday.

28 February The children still enjoy using different languages in the classroom. I am going to approach Mr Guhataour about coming into the classroom next week to make some booklets as we did in Urdu. I showed the children the Urdu–English nursery rhyme book and they were quite excited. I will also see Mrs Chaudry about coming in to read stories in Urdu again.

5 March We did some paired writing today and I noticed that some of the children who were less confident in English were conversing in the home language. We had quiet reading today and one boy asked me if he could look at a story pack I've compiled that has an accompanying tape in Urdu.

9 March This afternoon we looked at the number, colours and weather books in Urdu that had been made on the workshop day. The children who knew Urdu said the words in Urdu, and I said the English. They all really enjoyed looking at the books and I've left them on the book table for them to continue browsing when they want.

13 March The children really like the Urdu books and some even wanted to take them home. Mr Guhataour still hasn't helped with the Panjabi books and said he may not have the time, so I have asked Mrs Baig, who did the nursery book. Mrs Baig came in today of her own accord and still wants to do things in the classroom.

4 New arrivals

The early weeks in a new school in a new country can be traumatic. But adjustment to different styles of learning and teaching and different routines can be even more difficult when children need to operate in a new language.

It is also important to remember that new beginnings can take several different forms. Some children will be starting school in a new country for the first time. Others will be changing from one school to another, either because their parents have moved or because they are making the transition from infant to junior, or junior to secondary. Still others will be returning to school after an extended holiday in their home country. In all these cases, it is important to think of ways of making the experience as comfortable as possible.

A question of experience

Schools and teachers with little or no experience of beginner bilinguals often feel at sea when faced with new arrivals. They may be anxious to hand responsibility for the new arrivals' learning to a specialist support teacher and are dismayed if they find that this is not possible. In the absence of support staff, they often set out in search of resources which will offer structure to their teaching, only to be disappointed at the dearth of suitable materials.

When coming face to face with new arrivals, teachers sometimes offer inappropriate advice. They may, for instance, discourage the use of the first language and advise parents to use only English at home, unaware that this is unrealistic and potentially harmful. The main priority for teachers in cases of this kind is to acquire accurate information about language learning and bilingualism.

Teachers with limited experience of second language learners may not know that it is perfectly normal for children to spend weeks or even months quietly absorbing the sounds and patterns of the language before putting this new knowledge into practice. Teachers may feel that they are failing in their responsibilities when children make no attempt to speak. They may try to pressurize them into talking only to find that their efforts are counterproductive.

Classroom organization and pedagogy

The focus of this book, on ways in which children's first languages can be promoted in mainstream classrooms, in no way detracts from the central concern in multilingual classrooms to develop effective strategies for teaching English. Teachers are often unaware, for instance, of the impact of classroom organization on language learning. Children who are encouraged to work collaboratively in small groups have far more opportunities for speaking and listening to a range of native speakers than those in more traditional 'talk and chalk' classrooms where desks are arranged in rows and children are taught from the front. Similarly they may not realize the huge potential of the many everyday classroom activities – storytelling, games, role play and drama – which offer valuable support for language learning.

In this part of the book, we look at various matters of concern for new arrivals, including:

- ways of easing the transition in the early weeks at a new school, such as arranging for 'special friends', bilingual support and bilingual phrase books
- the needs of children returning from extended holidays in the home country.

Further reading

For a useful introduction to bilingualism, see:

- *A parents' and teachers' guide to bilingualism* by Colin Baker (Multilingual Matters, 1995)
- *The encyclopedia of bilingualism and bilingual education* by Colin Baker & Sylvia Price (Multilingual Matters, 1998).

For practical discussions of English language support, see:

- *Learning to learn in a second language* by Pauline Gibbons (Primary English Teaching Association, 1991; available in the UK from Bedfordshire Multicultural Resource Centre)
- *Speaking and listening in multilingual classrooms, Reading in multilingual classrooms* and *Writing in multilingual classrooms* by Viv Edwards (RALIC, 1995)
- *Supporting bilingual learners in schools* by Maggie Gravelle (Trentham, 1996)
- *New ways in teaching reading* edited by Richard Day, (TESOL, 1993)
- *New ways in teaching speaking* edited by K. Bailey & L. Savage (TESOL, 1994).

The early weeks

The stress of the early weeks can be reduced in many different ways, as we have seen already: a visual environment which reflects the cultures represented in the school can do a lot to minimize the feelings of strangeness on first entering the school; aspects of school organization, such as admissions procedures and home visits, can build important bridges between home and school. A range of strategies involving children's first languages can also help.

Special friends

In schools where there are other bilingual pupils, the transition can be eased with the support of children who speak the same language. A useful strategy is to introduce a special friend who can take care of the new child in the first few weeks, showing them where to go and inducting them into classroom and playground routines. Ideally, this friend should speak the same language as the newcomer, though a common language background is not a guarantee that children will get on. Personality also plays a role and it is important to choose someone who is open and friendly and enjoys responsibility.

Bilingual support

Songs, storytelling, listening to a tape which accompanies a picture book – all provide children with opportunities for listening to and absorbing the sounds and rhythms of a language without feeling any pressure to speak. But learning can be accelerated when the child receives bilingual support. Sometimes this will take the form of bilingual storytelling or listening to tapes that accompany dual language books (see pp. 60–61).

On other occasions, it will entail working alongside a bilingual support teacher.

Many mainstream teachers complain that they have little or no access to support teaching in either English or community languages. There are, however, alternative ways of offering bilingual support. Parents available in the day time may be prepared to help in the classroom. Those who work outside the home will be able to exchange important information with teachers when they drop off and pick up children; they may also be willing to help with translations at home. Older children in the school are another potential source of help.

Bilingual phrase books

Many schools have only the occasional child who arrives with little or no English. But in some schools there is a flow of newcomers throughout the year. Sometimes the children concerned are from refugee families; on other occasions, the school is close to the headquarters of a multinational organization, a university or a large hospital.

A bilingual phrase book can be a very useful prop for children in the early weeks in school. It usually consists of the English word or sentence, a translation and a transliteration. Sometimes children provide the accompanying illustrations. The transliteration helps the teacher attempt the other language when children themselves cannot read.

The first question to be considered is what should be included. Teachers can certainly make some intelligent guesses based on their own experience. But the final selection is likely to be more useful if the real experts are consulted. Why not

---

Fast I am asked my class teacher can I go tolett pleas and she sad yes I downt not English. and my teacher say on girl you explain. to Nadia Urdu and yougo with the Nadia and she sad yes and give me some books she sad right.

– *Nadia*

The first day I came to school. I need a pen, pencil, rubber and sharpener. My teacher give me these thing I can't speek English these way I asky my friend Urdu. I want a Genel work Book. Then my friend say to techer he want a book and my techer give me my dinner card and my friend say to me Urdu thats your dinner card and hometime my friend say that's hometime.

– *Sehrish*

Observations offered in the early months after arrival at Lea Junior School in Slough on the importance of friends

ask children who have been in the school a year or so to offer advice? Why not consult your dinner controllers?

The next decision concerns format. For instance, an A5 booklet is easily photocopied and not too cumbersome, while a laminated A4 card will stand up to the wear and tear of frequent use in the early weeks. There are, of course, many other possibilities. Whichever the format, an English template needs to be devised with ample space to add the other language and the transliteration.

While parents are the obvious people to provide the translations, a certain amount of sensitivity is required. Not everyone is literate in the language spoken at home. This problem can be overcome by asking parents if they – or someone they know – might be able to help with translation.

A request of this kind can be very helpful on a number of fronts. It provides an opportunity for making contact. It shows concern for children's welfare in the difficult early days. It also demonstrates an interest in the language and culture of the home. Most parents respond enthusiastically to requests of this kind.

The time initially invested in creating the English template reaps ample rewards. Once translated, the phrase book or card can be duplicated and reused by any other new arrivals.

The case studies which follow look at practical approaches to new beginnings: starting a new school in a new country; and changing from an infant to a junior school.

CASE STUDY: SURVIVING THE FIRST FEW WEEKS IN BINFIELD

Binfield Church of England Primary School receives children from families who come from all over the world to attend a nearby international college.

Lunchtime	
It is lunchtime now	现在是午饭时间
Have you got sandwiches?	你吃过三明治了吗
Have you got money?	你有零用钱吗?
I am a vegetarian	我是素食者.
Point to what you want	告诉我你要什么?

A page from a bilingual phrase book

Experience has taught Karen Vive, a teacher at the school, about the need to communicate basic information to the children, information that would keep them warm and safe and help them feel part of the school. Much can be done with the help of a confident friend, or with mimes and gestures, but not everything. To this end, she decided on a booklet of useful phrases which parents could translate and teachers transliterate for use in the early days.

Most of her initial research was carried out using simple questionnaires completed by other members of staff, including dinner controllers. There was a great deal of overlap in suggestions about what to include, making final selection a great deal easier. Older children willingly offered their opinions on the usefulness of the phrases in the booklet.

After an introductory session with parents, children are encouraged to familiarize themselves with the contents of the booklet in the more relaxed atmosphere of home.

CASE STUDY: THINKING ABOUT THE NEEDS OF NEW ARRIVALS

Helen MacDonald of Lea Junior School in Slough, where some 90 per cent of the children come from the Pakistani and Indian Panjab, approached the needs of new arrivals in a slightly different way.

Procedures are in place to ease each new cohort of children into the school and each new year group into their next classes. In this situation, most children have the support of their peers. But the child who arrives alone at any time in the school year from another country is in a very different situation.

I wanted to produce a booklet for the child to use at home before coming to school and also in the early days. I therefore spent time with small groups discussing how new arrivals might feel, what they would need and how present pupils might welcome them. I then asked them to write down suggestion for words and phrases (see the illustration below).

On reflection, I realized that a phrase book could provide an important means of communication between the new arrival and another child, even if there was no common language. Although it might be difficult to initiate a conversation 'cold', words and pictures relating to familiar things and places could help start a dialogue. Sharing the booklet would also provide the new child with individual attention.

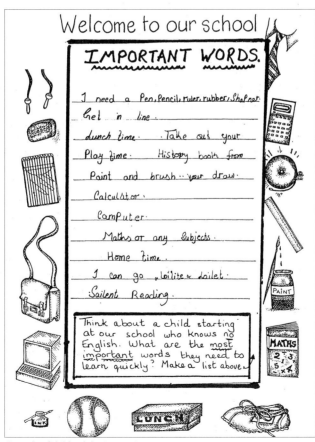

Example of children's brainstorming

CASE STUDY: A 'SURVIVAL KIT' FOR NEW ARRIVALS

As is often the case, the best information on what to include in a 'survival kit' for newcomers can be found by going directly to the experts: children and their parents who can still remember how they felt when they first arrived. Colleagues can also be a useful source of ideas for activities that work well and suggestions for the kind of background information which they would welcome.

Louise Evans and Zara Darchambaud, teachers in Cumnor Primary and St Michael's first School, two nearby schools, had similar concerns about families from many different parts of the world who come for relatively short periods to Oxford. They decided to work together to find solutions for shared problems and began by talking to colleagues, parents and children.

Colleagues were clear that they wanted practical ideas which they could put into practice immediately with new arrivals. They also wanted to explore how the schools could be more welcoming. The first step was to buy 'Welcome' posters in different languages to display in prominent positions. It was decided to approach parents about providing artefacts for the home corners. Ideas for working with new arrivals were shared.

Children were a useful source of information. Camille, a child from a French-German family, for instance, was happy to talk about what she had found helpful on arrival. She had enjoyed using a booklet, *All about me*, and making a simple bilingual picture dictionary.

Camille's mother was also consulted. She felt that the most useful information she had received was the name and phone number of the class 'link' parent who was able to offer help and advice outside school time.

These initial discussions helped to shape an action plan. They would:

- select and adapt materials from their own and other local schools for teachers to use with children
- produce with the help of children a simple class dictionary and personalized school timetables, plans and staff profiles
- produce an information pack for parents.

The original intention was that each teacher should have their own file but because this was too costly, reference copies were held centrally in the staff room.

The learning resources and information packs had obvious practical applications. Another benefit was the heightened awareness of bilingual learners' needs on the part of teachers, teaching assistants and dinner controllers. The involvement of bilingual children and their parents also made the project more valuable.

CASE STUDY: NEW BEGINNINGS

Montem School in Slough recently changed from being a Middle to a Junior School. The knowledge that they would be receiving two new intakes in the following September – Year 3 and Year 4 – served as a catalyst for looking very closely at ways in which children and their parents could be supported and welcomed into a new environment.

Anne Steele Arnett and Beverley Henry worked to develop a series of resources related to induction. They worked first on an activity sheet, to be used on the two induction days that the new intake spend with their teachers towards the end of the summer term. The sheet dealt with standard items required by the children – uniform, PE kit and writing equipment – and reinforced the start date and opening times for the new term. Parents were invited to an induction afternoon where staff were introduced and school routines explained in the home languages and English.

A school promotional video was made by children in the after school Video Club. This opened with a welcome in different languages,

My favourite activity this week was

اس ہفتے کا میرا پسندیدہ
سبق -

I have made friends with

میں نے ان بچوں سے دوستی کی -

My favourite lunch this week has been

اس ہفتے کا میرا پسندیدہ کھانا -

My favourite game in the playground has been

اس ہفتے کا میرا پسندیدہ کھیل

Extracts from the Montem induction booklet

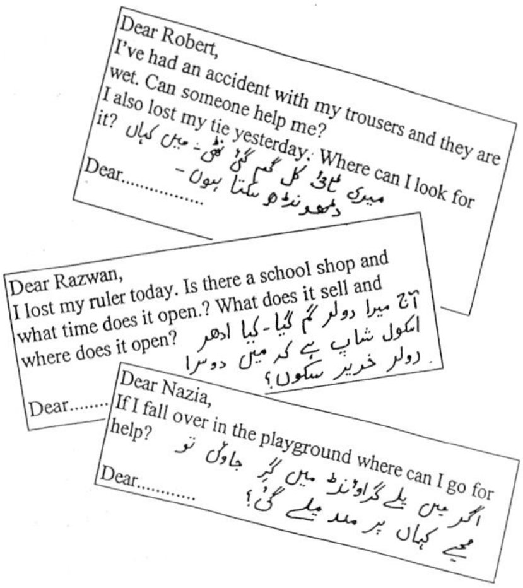

Dear Robert,
I've had an accident with my trousers and they are wet. Can someone help me?
I also lost my tie yesterday. Where can I look for it?

میری ٹائی کل گم ہو گئی تھی - میں کہاں اس
کو ڈھونڈ ہو سکتا ہوں -

Dear.................

Dear Razwan,
I lost my ruler today. Is there a school shop and what time does it open.? What does it sell and where does it open?

آج میرا رولر گم گیا - کیا ادھر
اسکول شاپ ہے کہ میں دوسرا
رولر خرید سکوں؟

Dear........

Dear Nazia,
If I fall over in the playground where can I go for help?

اگر میں پلے گراؤنڈ میں گر جاؤں تو
مجھے کہاں پر مدد ملے گی؟

Dear...........

Examples from an Agony Aunt/Uncle column

Finally, an induction booklet was developed for staff to use with their children over the first half term in school. The booklet was produced in dual language format and focused on the following topics:

- all about me
- my last school
- feeling welcome and making others feel welcome
- equipment and school bag
- classroom layout
- school plan
- timetable and what to remember each day
- matching activities with times of the day
- the school shop
- communicating politely
- lunchtime arrangements
- Friday focus: news about good things that have happened in the week (see illustration left)
- an Agony Aunt/Uncle column (see illustration above)

then featured eating arrangements, the library, playtimes, after school clubs, assemblies and the celebration of other religions and cultures, to name but a few of the items which children felt were important to document. Copies have been lodged in feeder schools to use as a backup for preliminary visits and also for loan to parents.

Extended visits

The needs of children departing for and returning from extended visits to their home country can be usefully considered at this point. Many families who have moved great distances can afford to make visits home only very occasionally and, for understandable reasons, wish to stay for an extended period before returning to their new country. This means that children may be away from school for many months, sometimes at a critical point in their development of English.

Consolidating first language skills

The early weeks following their return are often very difficult. Children may have lost a great deal of the fluency they had achieved in English before they left and may feel uncomfortable about needing to make major adjustments yet again. However, teachers need to remember that children's learning has not stood still. The time in the home country offers an opportunity to consolidate first language spoken skills and children who attend school also make valuable progress in literacy. They will in any case rapidly recover their fluency in English.

Extended visit packs

Teachers are anxious that children on extended visits should gain the maximum educational benefit. In an attempt to minimize the loss of English language skills, a number of LEAs have developed extended visit packs. Ideally, these are introduced to children and parents before they leave and completed during the time away. They serve the dual function of providing a chance to use English and making an interesting record of their stay which they can share on their return.

The project diary of Sue Budden, a teacher at Montem First School in Slough, includes references to her attempts to settle a child who has just returned from an extended visit to Pakistan.

31 January Today Kurram came back from Pakistan – he's been there since October. He came in and wouldn't speak to anyone. He didn't want to look at books – English or dual language – and just sat there staring out of the window. Then, when it was time for the register, I told the children to answer in their own languages as I thought this might make Kurram feel more at home. When it came to his name he answered in Urdu and from that point onwards seemed much happier. The children spoke to him in English and Urdu and he was soon working happily.

1 February Although Kurram has only just returned after a considerable time away I tried not to assume that he had forgotten everything and deliberately kept him in the same group as before he left. He has coped very well. If anything his handwriting has improved!

Details of extended visit materials are included in the AIMER database (see p.79)

5 Promoting spoken languages

Languages other than English are often invisible and inaudible in school. Children may deny knowledge of being able to speak or understand other languages; parents may say they speak only English at home. Sometimes, this is indeed the case: families have made a deliberate decision to shift from the community language to English. In other cases, however, such claims are – at best – a simplification of the truth. Even when English is the main language of communication, children will be privy to conversations in other languages with aunts, uncles, grandparents and friends and may have at least a passive understanding.

Protestations that English is the only language used in the home are sometimes a defence against the perceived negative attitudes of the school. Parents are still sometimes advised to speak English to their children – even in the face of overwhelming evidence of the importance of a solid foundation in the first language – and children are still discouraged from using their home language in either the classroom or the playground. It is not surprising that knowledge of other languages is underplayed.

Alternative approaches

Monolingual English-speaking teachers may feel ill-equipped to support children's use of home languages at school. They can, however, promote the status of bilingualism and bilingual pupils by working with bilingual colleagues and parents to use and develop their other languages.

In this part of the book, we look at ways of promoting spoken languages, including:

- bilingual stories and drama
- the use of audiovisual resources
- opportunities for language study where bilingual children are the experts.

Stories

The power of story – whether told or read – should never be underestimated. As well as helping us make sense of the world around us, it is a very effective prop for language learning. When the teacher reads a story, pictures offer visual support; when a teacher tells a story, the tone of voice, gesture and mime all help the audience understand what is taking place.

Bilingual stories

Bilingual stories can take a number of forms: they can be read from beginning to end first in one language, then in the other; or they can be read alternately page by page. The other language version can be read directly from the book or paraphrased. Questions and answers can be offered in both English and the minority language, ensuring maximum understanding of what the story is about. Stories in both languages can be brought to life by cut out pictures or magnet board figures.

Bilingual teachers are able to use both their languages. Monolingual teachers can involve bilingual colleagues or parents, as in Sue Budden's attempts to draw on the skills of parents on pp. 32–4. They can also use taped versions of the other language text, as in Ann Janes' account of making story cassettes on p. 48.

Bilingual storytelling is an enjoyable experience for monolingual English speakers and language learners alike: when children hear a story in two languages, the dominant language version offers valuable support for their understanding of the other language. This approach also creates opportunities for talking about the similarities and differences among languages.

Professional performers

Growing numbers of professionals bring a bilingual dimension to performance. Roop Singh, for instance, performs in English and Panjabi for school children all over the UK. He moulds his tales to the situation, delivering different versions of the same story according to the audience, which can range from nursery children to primary teachers attending INSET sessions.

He started his career by telling tales in English. On one occasion, however, when a teacher requested 'something different', he decided to tell the story of Jack and the beanstalk in Panjabi and was astonished at its success: the English-speaking members of the audience were able to follow from his gestures and, of course, their prior knowledge of the story. Since then, Roop Singh has usually told his tales in English and Panjabi, though some schools specifically request just Panjabi. He also offers storytelling workshops for children and storytelling art and craft sessions where children produce props to dramatize a story.

Some Theatre in Education companies such as M6 and the Half Moon Young People's Theatre now specialize in bilingual performance. M6, which operates within the North West Arts Board region, has included in its repertoire *Two days as a tiger* (Doh din kay shere), a play which uses Panjabi, Urdu and English. Productions from the London-based Half Moon Young People's Theatre have included *Kola Pata Bhut* (The hopscotch ghost), where actors move effortlessly from English to Bengali and Sylheti.

Audiovisual resources

Audiovisual resources give easy access to a range of other languages. They have the advantage of allowing children to work independently of the teacher, alone or in small groups, and are particularly valuable for monolingual teachers who wish to promote other languages. Resources produced either by commercial companies or with the help of children and parents can take a number of forms:

- Videocassette versions of children's stories in a number of languages.
- Tape cassette versions of stories and songs in English and a range of other languages.
- Tape-storypacks: children's story books to be used in conjunction with taped versions of the stories
- A small number of stories is available in different language versions – usually Spanish and Japanese for the US market – on CD-ROM. It is also possible to make your own recordings using hypertext.

- Interviews conducted by children as part of project work in English and in other languages.
- With encouragement, children rapidly become fascinated by the sounds of other languages and tapes can also be used as the basis for many different language study activities. For instance, listeners can be asked to identify the languages in short tape-recorded extracts. Rather than being expected to guess blind, this works better when children are given a choice of two languages.

Audiovisual resources require a carefully organized listening corner and a thoughtful approach to producing material for wider use. Chris Dickinson, a teacher-librarian at Thomas Buxton Junior School in East London has developed useful policies for both recording and organizing material and these form the basis for the guidelines which follow.

Organizing audiovisual resources

Storage

- The display and storage of headphones, cassette player and tapes in the listening area should be neat, attractive and easy to use.
- The use of nails, hooks, pegs or storage boxes may all help
- The cassette player should have a safe lockable place for the evening

Tape selection

- To ensure a good selection, tapes should be changed frequently from the library central stock.

Record keeping

- Records should be kept by the children or the teacher of tapes heard and by whom. This record could be in the form of a book, a card or a large chart.
- Care should be taken to make sure that all children have the same opportunities to hear tapes suitable for their particular needs, possibly by operating a rota.
- It is important to ensure that a child listening to a long story can reach the end before losing interest.

Training

- Children need to be reminded at regular intervals about how to use the listening area, eg how to return tapes to their cases correctly, the importance of keeping books and tapes together in their storage bags.
- All children need to know that damaged tapes or books, and storage bags with parts missing should be shown immediately to the class teacher and returned to the library.
- Children could be chosen for a set time to ensure that the listening corner is

tidy and to put away the tape recorder every evening.

Variety of use

The listening area may be used in many different ways:

- one or two children can listen to a tape and follow the book
- the whole class or a large group may listen to a tape supported by suitable visuals
- a child or small group can listen to a suitable tape as part of project work, eg transcribing an interview.

Variety of material

A listening area needs a variety of learning materials. Tapes can include non-fiction, poetry, rhymes, songs, music and quizzes.

Guidelines for producing tapes

Audience and purpose

Who is the listening material intended for and why?

Format

What length of tape is required? And how is the material to be organised, eg Bengali version on one side, English on the other, a different story on each side, story spread over two sides?

Presentation

What is the most effective way of presenting the material?

- one voice or more than one?
- is the pace appropriate for the age and ability level?
- are tones for turning pages required?
- is it necessary to have an introduction, music, sound effects or a conclusion?

End product

The finished tape needs to be played back to assess the quality of sound and content. It should also be trialled with its intended audience before:

- breaking the lugs on the tape so that it is impossible to record over the material
- labelling the tape and the case with number, title, author, indication of content and the school stamp
- placing the tape with any supporting materials such as books and pictures, in the correct storage bag or folder, which should be appropriately labelled and stamped
- producing a catalogue card for the school library
- making a copy of the tape and depositing the master copy in the library for safe keeping and further copying.

CASE STUDY: MAKING STORY CASSETTES IN OTHER LANGUAGES

Most of the bilingual children attending Bartlemas Nursery School in Oxford are Panjabi and Urdu speakers, though at various times they have also included speakers of a dozen other languages. Ann Janes describes a project to produce story cassettes in the full range of languages represented in the school.

In consultation with colleagues I chose several books which we read regularly in the nursery. Several Panjabi- and Urdu-speaking colleagues agreed to make recordings in their own time in the staff room. Initially we felt nervous about involving parents. Unsure about the technical aspects of the recording process, we didn't want to ask them to repeat the task if the tape was not of the required quality. However, as we have grown in confidence, this has ceased to be an issue.

The tapes were recorded using a tape recorder with a built-in microphone which offers adequate but not outstanding sound quality reproduction. A recorder with a separate microphone would definitely have been preferable. To add authenticity, I struck a triangle to make the ping sound that you hear on commercial tapes as a cue for children to turn the page!

We currently have some fourteen tapes in English, Urdu, Panjabi, Russian and Bengali and plan to expand the range of languages over time. The tapes have the whole story in the minority language on one side and English on the other. However, I also plan to experiment with producing tapes where each page is read first in one language, then in the other. In this way bilingual and monolingual children can listen together; the first language will also reinforce the English in the case of bilingual children.

I wanted to use story props with the books and tapes. I selected pictures, games and sequencing cards to accompany the stories we had chosen from the range produced by the Tower Hamlets Language Support Service. I also wanted to involve parents in making the props and organized a workshop, complete with toys for toddlers and refreshments.

I have already been able to use the tapes in interesting ways. I have attempted bilingual storytelling at group time by pausing a Panjabi tape at the 'ping'. I also hope to make copies of the tapes for children to borrow and listen to at home, something which will be of special benefit to parents who speak or read little English.

Looking back on our efforts this term, it has proved relatively simple to build up a valuable resource base which will be of benefit to all the children in the nursery at far less expense than buying commercial tapes. I had also completely underestimated the enthusiasm of staff and parents.

CASE STUDY: ORAL HISTORY INTERVIEWS

Karen Wright, working with Year 6 children at Godolphin Junior School, attached great importance to oral history in topic work on Slough since 1950. Over 90 per cent of the families of children at the school had come from the Indian sub-continent and most of these were Panjabi/Urdu speakers.

The original intention was to video interviews with parents in the classroom, but problems soon became apparent. Children reported that their parents were unwilling or unable to come into school; one boy gave a further clue to the problem when he added that only little children have their parents in the classroom.

The solution emerged when several children volunteered to do taped interviews with parents in the home. Questions and answers on the circumstances surrounding families' arrival in Slough were offered in English, Panjabi and Urdu and played back to all the children in a history class. The embarrassment and self-consciousness which had been very much in evidence at the beginning of the project rapidly gave way to interest and excitement. The interviews yielded valuable information on local history; they also served as a stimulus for discussing language.

Further reading

For a powerful approach to the development of children's historical thinking which is especially sensitive to the needs of bilingual children, see *Speaking about the past* by Sandip Hazareesingh (Trentham books, 1994).

Language study

Bilingual learners are an invaluable teaching resource. Children who speak other languages are able to model the enormous variety of sounds and structures which characterize human language. They underline the fact that there are many different ways of categorizing and representing our experiences of life. At the same time, they remind us of the many similarities which link languages as geographically distant as Gaelic and Gujarati.

Equally important, bilingual learners serve as a catalyst for discussing the social and political dimensions – the fact that language and identity are inextricably linked. Bangladeshi children, for instance, will know about the language martyrs who gave their lives in the struggle for independence. Children from the former Yugoslavia will be able to explain that the Orthodox Serbs write their language in the Cyrillic script while the Catholic Croatians use the Roman alphabet.

Bilingual learners will be able to talk with authority about 'code-switching' between one language and another. Many will have direct experience of the communication problems that arise with grandparents and relatives from the home country when children born abroad fail to maintain their first languages. Many will also be able to explain what takes place in community language classes. In the process, monolingual peers begin to understand the linguistic achievements of bilingual classmates and the importance of other languages in their lives. Bilingual children assume expert status.

The case studies which follow explore various attempts to draw on the expertise of bilingual children in the class in speaking other languages.

CASE STUDY: CHILDREN AS TEACHERS: WHERE IN THE WORLD?

A 'Where in the world week' at Godolphin Junior School in Slough, which focused on different countries for a set period every day, served as a springboard for Candy Mole to explore possibilities for using other languages with children, most of whom come from Panjabi- and Urdu-speaking families.

As part of our work on European languages, the children used dictionaries to find the French, German, Italian and Spanish for basic words such as hello, goodbye, please and thank you. Urdu- and Panjabi-speaking children spontaneously offered the same words in their languages. Everyone was eager to practise their new vocabulary as they – or anyone else – entered or left the classroom.

Answering the register also provided opportunities for using other languages. In Candy's class, the girls are listed first and children call out their number. By the end of 'Where in the world week', the children began to use the language of their choice – French, German or Urdu/Panjabi – when they responded. The girls initially showed more enthusiasm than the boys, partly perhaps because they were more extrovert but also because the boys' numbers fell between 21 and 34 and many simply did not know the higher numbers in any language other than English. However, within a few days, several of the boys had asked for or found out their number in another language and were joining in with the rest of the class.

One group of children made a set of paired cards using numbers from one to ten in Urdu, Panjabi, French and German. The success of this game served as a catalyst for making number mobiles in design and technology lessons, with children using their language of choice – this time English, French, German, Hindi, Panjabi and Urdu. On one occasion, a group which included both Indian Sikh and Pakistani Muslim children decided without prompting to write one to five in Nastaliq script for Urdu and six to ten in Gurmukhi script for Panjabi.

At the end of term, children were given printed copies of colour names and days of the week in Urdu and Panjabi to decorate for homework. The response was enthusiastic and their efforts were incorporated into a display on their return to school.

The introduction of a new topic on weather provided another opportunity to use home languages in classroom displays. Information collected by the children on wind speed and direction, rainfall and clouds was recorded on a display board which also included Panjabi and Urdu weather charts illustrating sun, cloud, fog, wind and rain.

The impact on the class is ongoing. Children are now much more confident about using their home languages in school. They always respond enthusiastically to their teacher's attempts to use Urdu and Panjabi and often bring in work which they have done at the mosque, Gurdwara or at home. Monolingual English speakers, too, have shown excitement and pride in using other languages and there has been a growth in language awareness.

CASE STUDY: MY TEACHER, BASHIR

Anna Ljumovic and Farzana Akbar worked on a project on 'Knowledge about language' with a Year 10 class in Lanfranc High School in Croydon which included twelve bilingual pupils who spoke between them ten languages in addition to English.

The class was divided into groups taking into account factors such as gender and length of time learning English. Each group was 'taught' by a bilingual student who determined which language would be studied.

The learning targets for the new language were:

- to count up to 20
- to hold a simple conversation
- to recite a rhyme or poem.

Teachers in their new role as observers became aware of both the monolingual pupils' embarrassment at being unable to pronounce words correctly and of their admiration for the skills of their bilingual peers. Pupils were also fascinated by both the differences and the similarities between the target language and English.

The benefits for 'teachers' and students were very clear. 'Teachers' became more aware by having to make explicit their own knowledge of their language. Students not only became more aware of language but often expressed more positive attitudes to their bilingual class mates. This development was very clear in a written assignment submitted by a boy who had initially been hostile to the project:

'No one had a bad word to say about their teacher nor the language they had learned. Normally foreign people from India, France and Pakistan stay quiet but through this they have helped to take control of the situation. I would like to thank my teacher who taught me his language, Bashir.'

6 Reading in other languages

Bilingual children's experiences of reading vary a great deal. The very young, children who have not previously attended school, and children whose education has been interrupted by war will have limited exposure to the written word. Children who have been to school in the home country may have well-developed literacy skills in the community language, and varying levels of experience with print in English. Children born in the new country will be able to read and write English but will have acquired literacy skills in the community language only if they have attended classes or received a great deal of support at home.

Transfer of skills

We know that a good foundation in the first language is extremely helpful in learning to read and write second and subsequent languages. Traditionally, the focus for children arriving in an English-speaking school system was on the acquisition of literacy in English – time was in too short a supply to consider maintaining or developing literacy in another language. New understandings of the nature of language and learning have caused us to reappraise this situation: children are well able to read and write in two – and more – languages.

Additional language learners with experience of the roman alphabet will find themselves at an initial advantage in learning to read other languages which also use the roman alphabet. However, fluent readers use similar strategies, irrespective of the writing system: children who are already literate in one language will be able to transfer a whole range of skills when they start to read a second language. They know, for instance, that print carries meaning, that the stream of print is broken into words and that there are certain rules and expectations about how print is laid out on the page. They also understand that it is possible to skip inessential words, to guess unknown words from context and to read ahead when you don't know a word.

Bilingual support

Bilingual teachers, support teachers, classroom assistants and parents are obviously well-placed to encourage children's literacy development in both languages. They can check whether children have understood what they are reading and short-circuit frustration by providing the word or expression in the other language. They are also able to explore feelings and experiences which grow out of the text, and to encourage children to make inferences.

Monolingual teachers

Monolingual English-speaking teachers are clearly more limited in the support which they can offer. None the less, they can promote multiple literacies in a number of ways. For instance, they can give a high profile to books, dictionaries and posters in single and dual language format, as well as encouraging children to make, read and share books in other languages with the help of bilingual adults and more experienced peers. Expressions of interest in children's achievements outside school on the part of monolingual teachers can also motivate children to maintain progress in the community language.

Ik lees graag

Ik heet Irene en ik lees graag.
Ik lees graag lange boeken

Ik lees graag korte boeken

Ik lees graag grappige boeken

Ik lees graag verdrietige
boeken

Ik lees graag boeken met
plaatjes

Ik lees gewoon graag

'I like reading': a story in Dutch

The knowledge that a child is already literate in another language has obvious implications for the choice of teaching strategies and materials. Admission forms should actively seek information on children's experience of literacy in all their languages. Assessment information should also automatically record children's progress in all languages.

Simulating reading in another language

When used by individuals or groups of teachers, the Dutch 'story' (see left) shows clearly the kinds of strategy which we bring to reading a text in an unfamiliar language. It demonstrates the importance of the visual support offered by the illustrations; the use of repetition; and words which are similar in English or other languages we may know. It also helps to highlight aspects of a text which support both beginner bilinguals and beginner readers. finally, it reminds us of the many advantages which children already literate in another language bring to the task of learning to read English.

This exercise has been used very successfully to help groups of teachers focus on the needs of children reading in a second language. It can also be used to encourage children to think about the different cues we use when learning to read and to highlight the skills of bilingual readers.

In this part of the book we look at various ways in which an understanding of children's previous experiences has implications for the teaching of reading, including:

- the influence of culture on how we interact with text
- the importance of appropriate resources.

Reading and culture

Traditionally, learning to read was seen in terms of acquiring a set of skills which allowed us to decode the written word. More recently, we have come to realize that reading entails making meaning out of print: children need to learn strategies which allow them to draw on their knowledge of language, life and books to predict what lies ahead. However, the story doesn't finish here. There is also a growing understanding that ways of interacting with print are determined to a large extent by cultural expectations (Heath, 1983; Baynham, 1995; Gregory, 1996).

Children who attend mosque classes, for instance, recite passages which they learn by heart. Many community language classes adhere closely to the pattern: demonstrate, repeat, practise, test. All these activities are far removed from the emphasis on environmental print and prediction and reading for enjoyment which characterize many classrooms in the English-speaking world.

The value of literacy

Many children spend a great deal of time learning to read and write their community languages in classes outside school. While literacy is a highly prized activity in most societies, the precise nature of the relationship with print varies. In communities where literacy is closely linked with religion, holy texts are treated with reverence and readers are sometimes required to wash before opening the pages. Often great importance is attached to a literal interpretation of the text. Sometimes books are offered as a reward for achievement rather than as an enticement to learn. In many communities reading is a social activity – a letter or newspaper will be read aloud and the meaning negotiated within the group – and individuals who immerse themselves for long periods in a book are considered anti-social.

The teacher's responsibilities

A multilingual classroom will include children with many different experiences of literacy. This is not necessarily a problem. Different families operate with different rules but children visiting or playing with friends rapidly adjust to the expectations of the host family. In the same way, children seem to accommodate with little difficulty to the different rules which operate, on the one hand, in school and, on the other, in community classes.

Difficulties are more likely to arise on the level of parents and teachers. When the school's approach to reading is very different from the one with which parents are familiar, it is not surprising that they should feel a level of discomfort, as illustrated in the case study on p.56.

It is essential that teachers appreciate that their approach to the teaching of reading is one among many. While it is clearly impractical to adopt different approaches for different children, it can be helpful to use a variety of approaches with all children: in this way they extend their experiences of learning in different contexts and for different purposes. Teachers also have a responsibility to explain to parents precisely how they approach the teaching of reading – and why. Parents will not necessarily agree that the school's way is better than their own, but they are likely to feel much happier when they understand the reasons.

There are many opportunities for teachers to make clear how they approach the teaching of reading: curriculum evenings

Extract from a booklet for parents on reading produced by Thomas Buxton Junior School, East London.

for parents; information booklets, preferably in the main minority language(s) of the school as well as English; informal gatherings such as parent and toddler mornings or book and toy library sessions; and videos with commentary in appropriate languages.

The role of siblings

More recently, the work of Eve Gregory (1997) has highlighted the critical role of siblings in the reading development of many second language learners. Close observation of reading in the home of Bangladeshi children has shown that, while mothers help children practise from their Bengali primers and recite prayers in Arabic, they usually play no part in their children's reading in English. The reasons are various: mothers express confidence in the children's teachers; often their own English is limited; some are also mystified that their children's reading books have no clear moral or religious purpose.

In the Bangladeshi community it would seem that siblings, rather than parents, take the main responsibility for hearing children read. They provide scaffolding which is closely adjusted to the reading ability of the individual they are helping, using a complex blend of Qu'ránic and school practices. For instance, children often listen and repeat in a way which is highly reminiscent of mosque and Bengali classes. However, siblings do not insist on accuracy and children are free to predict the next piece of text. Eve Gregory concludes that a more detailed knowledge of reading practices at home might help teachers build more successfully on children's existing strategies.

In short, it is important both for teachers to understand the approaches to literacy of different minority communities and for families to understand what is happening in school. Together, parents and teachers make a powerful team.

The case studies which follow all highlight the importance of a wider perspective on children's development as readers. Issues raised include misunderstandings which take place when teachers assume that their approach to literacy is the only one and fail to explain how the school's perspective; the potential for harnessing the enthusiasm of older siblings in literacy development; and opportunities for peer tutoring in reading in two languages.

CASE STUDY: HE CAN'T EVEN WRITE HIS NAME!

Eve Gregory describes attempts to understand why Tony, a little boy whose family had come from Hong Kong, failed to thrive on starting school.

Tony's family comes from Hong Kong. He has recently started school, having received no nursery education and understanding very little English. He also attends a Saturday school where he is learning to become literate in Mandarin.

Tony's father didn't foresee any difficulty for him in learning to read and write in two languages simultaneously. Initially he welcomed Tony's teacher warmly and spoke to her enthusiastically about helping at home.

Three months later, it is clear that Tony is experiencing difficulties in settling into school. His teacher is frustrated that he does not want to choose attractive storybooks to read with her. Nor does he include predicting the story within his interpretation of reading. Tony rather expects to describe the illustrations by labelling the figures or objects depicted. He focuses on individual words: for Tony it is important to get them right through constant repetition and questioning.

'Tony can't have this book yet. You must keep it and give it to him later.'

'But why?'

'Because he can't read the words. First he must read the words, then he can have the book.'

Tony's grandfather pulls out an exercise book from under the counter and shows it to the teacher. A number of pages have been filled with immaculate ideographs. His grandfather says proudly that Tony has completed these at Chinese Saturday school. With a sceptical look at the teacher, he pulls out a screwed up piece of paper. On one side is a shop advertisement from which it had been recycled. On the other is a drawing of a transformer. Tony's grandfather:

'This is from his English school. This is rubbish.'

Pointing to the corner where 'ToNy' is written, he says,

'Look. He can't even write his name yet!'

In order to understand the reactions of Tony and his family, it is important to appreciate their very different experiences of the written word. In Saturday school, children divide the page of an exercise book into columns and practise ideographs over and over again until they are perfect. Attention to detail is particularly important, for the misplacing or omission of a single stroke will completely change the meaning of the symbol. Tony learns to read by reciting individual words after the teacher in chorus with the other children. Children sit in rows. There is no choice of activity and they receive homework from the very start. There is no talk to other children or to the teacher unless requested.

Chinese families usually hold books in the highest esteem, but believe that children must prove themselves worthy of receiving them by first learning how to read. To have immediate access to books devalues both the book and the principle of hard work.

This case study has been abridged from Gregory (1993).

CASE STUDY: CHILDREN AS READING TEACHERS

Sue Wilks has developed paired reading in exciting new directions at Nelson Mandela School in Birmingham. The school had a history of success in building good links with families from minority communities, but found it difficult to persuade parents to help with children's learning at home, partly no doubt because they lacked confidence and partly because of the strong cultural belief that school is the proper place for learning.

The obvious way forward was to extend the paired reading which was already taking place between infant and junior classes to siblings in the home. The response was enthusiastic. Sue Wilks called a meeting for any child interested in helping a younger brother or sister with reading. It was decided that 'teachers' would spend time reading with a sibling during the daily ERIC (Everyone Reading in Class) session. Children also made a commitment to hear their siblings reading at home and to record progress in a special file. The 'teachers' would be rewarded for their efforts with a certificate when their 'student' made a measured amount of progress.

Children were soon exchanging opinions and offering advice at a twice weekly lunchtime meetings of the Young Teachers' Club. Topics of conversation included whether it was better for evening teaching sessions to take place before or after mosque class, and whether it was OK to persuade the 'student' to cooperate with a sweet. Children also made simple equipment that could be borrowed to use at home.

The Young Teachers' Club attracted children of all kinds. There were approximately equal numbers of girls and boys. Some of the volunteers were themselves experiencing learning difficulties but, like all the others in the project, they clearly gained a great deal of confidence from their new role.

The scheme has grown to include an astonishing 119 'teachers'. The only note of dissent has been from parents with just one child at the school, who feel that they are missing out. The school's response has been to find friends or neighbours who could help.

The benefits are beginning to emerge. Over a third of the school's seven year olds – all second language learners – achieved level 3 (above average) in reading in national curriculum tests.

CASE STUDY: PAIRED READING IN TWO LANGUAGES

For a full account of this project see Lamey (1989).

Jim Lamey, a teacher in a boys' comprehensive school in the East End of London embarked with Eamon Helly, a language support teacher, on a paired reading project in a Year 9 class where 95 per cent of the pupils were Bangladeshis. The aim was to make the students teachers of reading, where possible in two languages.

The project began with a class discussion on the importance of reading. Children brainstormed their ideas which were then translated by a fluent bilingual student. Ideas were copied into their Paired Reading folders. The class was then divided into groups of four or five, to discuss how they could help each

other improve their reading, and ideas were pooled in whole class discussion. The following guidelines emerged – with support from their teachers – and were reproduced as a wall poster and placed in their Paired Reading folders:

- I should give my partner the chance to say the word again and get it right
- I should only correct my partner if what he has said changes the meaning of a sentence as it appears in the book
- I should only give my partner a word if I am certain he does not know it.

- I should talk to my partner in English/Bengali and ask him questions to try to get him to guess the word he has got wrong
- I should help my partner by pointing to pictures in the story
- I should help my partner to understand the story by acting it out
- I should praise my partner when he gets something right.

The guidelines were translated into Sylheti for the benefit of the newer arrivals.

The success of the project can be illustrated by recorded extracts from one of the partnerships. Shalim Ahmed is a beginner bilingual, only able to read simple texts in English, but is a competent reader in Bengali. Enamul Goni copes well with reading in English but his literacy skills in Bengali are more limited than his partner's. When reading the sentence, 'They wished each other good day', the following conversation ensued:

S: They washed
E: (in Sylheti) No. If you don't have enough money... what do you do?
S: (in Sylheti) You wish for some.
E: (in Sylheti) What is this in English?

S: Wish
E: (in Sylheti) Try the sentence again.
S: They wished each other a good day.

Later; when Shalim reads, 'He hummed a pleasant tune', Enamul checks to make sure he has understood:

E: (in Sylheti) What does pleasant (said in English) mean?
S: (in Sylheti) Very noisy.
E: No. Pleasant (said in English) means nice.

The benefits of bilingual support are evident in these exchanges. By asking questions in Sylheti – and where necessary, providing translations of unfamiliar words, Enamul is able to make sure that Shalim understands what he is reading. When the boys changed roles, a Bengali-speaking colleague was able to confirm that Shalim supported Enamul in the same way. This more active role within the classroom also increased his status with his peers.

The boys were enthusiastic about paired reading: almost all felt that their English reading had improved and almost half said that they had made progress in Bengali.

Resources

There are several things to consider when choosing books for bilingual readers, whether in English or community languages.

Books in English

In the case of beginner bilinguals, books in English need to be culturally sensitive. Many teachers are aware of common areas of difficulty. For instance, *Charlotte's Web* – where the central character is a pig – would not be a good choice for a class reader in a school with a high proportion of Muslims. Many Pakistani children find pigs so offensive that they will not even say the word, referring instead to the 'p-i-g' word.

It is also useful to be aware of different cultural connotations: in the Indian subcontinent, the owl is associated with stupidity, not wisdom. This information can transform the understanding of books, from *Winnie the Pooh* to *Owl babies*.

Ideally books should deal with issues which will be accessible to children with limited experience of life in the new country. When we are unfamiliar with a concept such as hitchhiking or bridesmaids we can be so disorientated that none of the story makes sense.

It goes without saying that books need to present positive images of people from different cultural backgrounds. In the past this was a real problem. Non-white children were often absent, made a token appearance, or were presented in a stereotypical way, such as the black boy good at sports or the African cannibal. The number of books with strong African-American and African-Caribbean characters has greatly increased in recent years. However, books with strong Asian characters are still relatively rare, except in books imported from the Indian subcontinent. The same is true of Chinese characters.

Bilingual readers need books with a high level of visual support which will help them to cue into what the text is all about. They also need books that support their language development: repetition, rhythm and rhyme will help them to internalize the vocabulary and structures of English, as well as to predict what comes next.

Older bilingual readers have additional needs. It is important that the books they read are not too babyish, either in subject matter or in the style of illustrations and format. Often, if there is a strong element of humour, the book will appeal to a much wider age group.

Single language books

The presence of books in other languages makes it clear to bilingual children that the school values linguistic diversity. It also raises monolingual children's awareness of other languages and scripts.

Specialist bookshops that import books from the country of origin are an important sources of other language materials. It is also possible to find different language versions of the same book. For instance, Learning Media produce a range of books in Maori and other Pacific languages for the New Zealand government. Child's Play, a British publisher, produces several titles in half a dozen European languages. Partnership Publishing produces Urdu and English versions of *The balloon detectives* (Jones, 1996). Some governments fund the publication of learning materials for children overseas: this is the case, for instance, with Italian textbooks in Canada, and books for the Hong Kong Chinese in Britain, while the overseas version of *The People's Daily*, a weekly newspaper for the Chinese abroad, has a weekly lesson for young learners. Small community publishers such as Mantra and Magi produce books in other languages. And many teachers, parents and children are involved in the small-scale production of books in other languages.

A Chinese lesson from *The People's Daily*.

Problems with imported books

While multilingual resources are an undoubted asset for any classroom, some teachers express reservations. Books produced abroad often deal with events outside the experience of children born in the new country.

There are also problems with language level. A book designed, say, for a ten year old child in Italy may be far too difficult for a Italian child born abroad. But, by the same token, books written at an appropriate linguistic level for children born overseas may seem very babyish.

Some teachers also complain that the production standards are lower in books from overseas, particularly the Indian sub-continent, and that this may send negative messages to children about their status. It seems, though, that this concern may be unfounded. The Multilingual Resources for Children Project (1995) found that children make judgements about materials on the basis of many variables, including subject and style of illustration. Equally important, many children reacted favourably to the Indian 'feel' of some books.

Dual language books

Dual language books have been a feature of many classrooms for a number of years. One of the aims is to raise the status of other languages and scripts though, ironically, badly designed dual language books may have the opposite effect. When a second language is added there are many pitfalls. The size, weight and spacing of the two languages may make one language seem more important than the other. The relationship of the two languages to the illustrations may also pose questions about the relative status of the languages, or cause overcrowding on the page.

When two languages run in different directions, one script usually takes precedence – in most Urdu–English dual language books, for instance, the page numbering runs from left to right. There are, however, many ingenious solutions for this problem. *The moving mango tree and other tales* by Zohra Jabeen (Partnership Teaching, 1992) contains two separate books within the same cover, the English version on the left hand side and the Urdu on the right. Illustrations appear at the appropriate place across all four pages visible at any one time. *Send for Sohail* by Grange Road First School, Bradford (Partnership Publishing, 1993) uses another approach: on each double page spread, the illustration is set above two columns of text – the English on the left, the Urdu on the right. Zigzag books provide yet another solution: English can run from left to right on one side; Urdu from right to left on the other.

Other challenges for dual texts include the quality of the translation (sometimes the community language text is more difficult than the English) and the suitability of the topic (some subjects make the journey from one language to

A page from The great escape, a wordless picture book by Phillipe Dupasquier (Walker, 1989)

another rather better than others). Yet in spite of criticisms of this kind, dual texts represent a very valuable way of keeping other languages in high profile; they also offer useful opportunities for teachers to encourage children's biliterate development.

Ways of reading dual texts

Dual texts tend to be more popular in mainstream than in community schools. Many bilingual parents and teachers dislike dual language books. They suspect that when children are faced with the two languages, they will always choose the English text. However, this is only part of the story. Although some English-dominant children consulted by the Multilingual Resources for Children Project (1995) admitted that they only read the English, there was evidence of many different approaches to dual texts. New arrivals, for instance, use the second language to help with the English. Well-established bilinguals often read the community language, using the English to help them when they reach an unfamiliar word. Monolingual English speakers also enjoy 'reading' dual language books either on their own or alongside a bilingual reader, making interesting hypotheses about similarities and differences between English and the other language.

Wordless picture books

Another genre deserves special mention at this point. Wordless picture books are a very useful way into early reading. They tell a story through a series of pictures. You can use the pictures to get the reader to look ahead and predict the outcome of the story. You can also use them to explain culture-specific references in the pictures. They help develop an understanding of fundamental features of story, like sequence and climax. One of the strongest points about wordless picture books is that children can be confident that their version of the story is valid. And, very significant for the present discussion, they can be used for telling stories in English or the community language.

Wordless big books – now available in increasing numbers – also offer opportunities for shared writing. The SRA McGraw Hill *Stick-on storybooks: wordless books to write and read* series, for instance, exploits this potential by providing self-adhesive writing paper which allows children to write or dictate their story. When the paper is removed a new story can be created.

Further reading

- *Building bridges* by the Multilingual Resources for Children Project (Multilingual Matters, 1995)
- For a range of practical ideas on arrangements which give scripts with different directionality equal status, see: *Write around the world* by Sue Walker, Viv Edwards & Heather Leonard (RALIC, 1998).

The case studies which follow look at a range of activities around books, including the evaluation of resources, opportunities for language learning related to well-known children's books and book making.

CASE STUDY: A RESOURCES AUDIT

It is important to have as full as possible an overview of the resources currently available in the school in order to identify weaknesses and gaps. Bilingual colleagues can play a particularly important role in evaluating books in other languages.

Carol Templeman of Slough Centre Nursery School wanted to assess and update the book stock in her school. Before she could embark on this task, however, she felt the need to research and prepare a policy for the selection of books which could be agreed by the whole staff.

Carol compiled a questionnaire to collect information and ideas for later discussion at a staff consultation meeting. When a draft policy had been agreed, she began an audit of almost 1,000 books, a very time-consuming process. Books were assessed against the school policy on illustrations, storyline, quality of printing, language and dual text status issues.

She paid particular attention to stereotyping, inaccuracy and caricature and looked for interesting, relevant subjects with plenty

of realism. Decisions were very much informed by the findings of a language survey undertaken by a colleague. She also looked closely at the books' age and physical condition.

She removed approximately a quarter of the books and relegated some others to a store room so that she could seek the opinion of her colleagues. She also enlisted the help of bilingual colleagues in assessing the quality of translation and the suitability of the dual language books.

Next came the search for new resources. She sent for catalogues from community language publishers and visited some specialist bookshops. It soon became apparent that certain markets were better provided than others. For instance, there was a wide selection of books featuring African-Caribbean and African-American characters and authors, but relatively few positive books meeting the needs of – or written by – members of Asian communities.

Carol organized displays or visits from several specialist publishers and book suppliers as part of the school open day, an initiative which was greeted with enthusiasm by staff and parents. She also exchanged some 80 books for more appropriate titles from the School Library Service.

On reflection she feels the key issue is the importance of a whole school policy to ensure consistency and appropriate selection. She is also convinced of the painful need to scrap old stock which is no longer appropriate. She thinks there should be regular stock review backed by suitable levels of funding and regular visits to the School Library Service to change and update the school's selection.

CASE STUDY: CHILDREN AS CRITICS

Jagiro Goodwin and Angela Wellings tackle a similar issue – but with the help of Year 5 and 6 children in Wilson Primary School in Reading.

As part of the school action plan on education for equality, staff had identified the evaluation and update of resources in the library. The humanities section was the starting point as this was thought to be the area most prone to stereotyping. We were given responsibility for the evaluation and it was not long before we made the decision that it would be challenging for us and for the children if we undertook the task together. Each week for six weeks, we worked with a different group of twelve children.

If we were to help the children detect bias and stereotypes in books, we needed to begin by establishing the stereotypes they already held. We started by brainstorming on the Australian soap, Neighbours, before moving on to 'The continent of Africa'.

The brainstorming allowed us to lead into a lengthy discussion of questions such as:

- What is a stereotype?
- What kinds of stereotypes are there?
- Where do stereotypes come from and how do we learn them?

Evaluating the books

The next activity was done in pairs. Each pair was given a book from the humanities section of the library and given about forty minutes for the evaluation.

Each pair then spent the first few minutes scanning the book to get a flavour of its contents before using the questionnaire (see left) to examine it in greater detail. As we moved around the room we were aware of some quite heated discussion. Children put their points of view, showed disapproval when materials were especially negative, negotiated at quite a

Title of book:

Look carefully at:
- the illustrations
- the text

then write your comments in the boxes below.

	Positive	Negative
Facial features		
Dress		
Housing		
Rich/poor		
Relationships with white people		
Language – the words used to describe black people		

Other observations: are any groups of people missing from the book? If so, who are they and why do you think they have been left out?

A questionnaire for evaluating the books

sophisticated level and, in most cases, reached a consensus about the books.

The group came back together at the end of the session to report on their findings. We formed a large circle and invited one member from each pair to describe the book while a teacher acted as scribe.

As a general rule, books containing photographs were viewed more positively than books with illustrations. A book on China caused particular offence: 'This book makes everyone look the same' and 'It's not true that Chinese people have yellow skin.' Similarly, books which portrayed only one perspective were criticized: 'This book shows that people in England are rich and that's not true.' The children also detected bias by omission and the use of inaccurate names.

The activity ended with a discussion about what should happen to the books. We operated a voting system whereby if the majority of the group found a book offensive and believed it had no place in the school library, then it should be removed.

CASE STUDY: LANGUAGE ACTIVITIES USING BOOKS

Ren Thurston set out to make language resources directly related to texts for use by early years teachers in SS Mary and John School, Oxford. The activities which she developed offered scaffolding for children's learning of English; they also created opportunities for sharing information on their first languages.

Ren chose *Dear Zoo* as her first story, tracing, colouring and laminating the pairs of animals. The children used the animals in retelling the story, playing Snap and Pelmanism, extending the storyline and presenting alternative versions. Bilingual children quickly learned the animal names in English, something which helped their confidence in talking about and retelling the story. Mohshina joined in enthusiastically with, 'I send back' which was finally modified to, 'I sent him back' as she listened to her English users' model.

Where's Spot? by Eric Hill also features animal characters and a predictable, repetitive text. It offers many opportunities for learning prepositions. This time follow-up activities took the form of a game with lift-up flaps asking questions such as, 'Where are the animals hiding?' and 'Who is hiding behind the door?' with the answers revealed under the flap. Hisyam, recently arrived from Malaysia, could not disguise his delight at the interactive nature of the book and game, and there was renewed enthusiasm for the Spot programme on the classroom computer.

Geographical terms such as mountain, jungle, river, sea and beach were discussed naturally and repetitively as children made a three dimensional model of the tropical paradise visited by *The little polar bear*. As they worked in small groups to make the features out of mod-rock and newspaper, the bilingual children not only learned the relevant vocabulary in English but also taught equivalents in their own language to the others. Children retold and extended the story using plastic animals.

The snowman was chosen in the knowledge that many of the children had already seen the video. The beginning – where the boy wakes, realizes it is snowing, rushes to get dressed and go out – makes a perfect sequencing activity, using two colour photocopies of the page before cutting up and laminating the individual frames. When telling the story in pairs, the English-speaking children inevitably took the lead, but bilingual children took an active part in follow-up activities, pointing and moving cards around. This was a very popular activity which generated a lot of discussion. Games of Pelmanism and Snap were also played.

All these activities provided a highly motivating and enjoyable context for language learning. Children remained on task and used the resources with considerable imagination. Fluent English speakers were able in a natural and unthreatening way to help bilingual learners articulate their ideas. Bilingual learners, for their part, were able to take risks, demonstrate their understanding, and take an active part in their own learning. They are returning to the texts with delight and confidence. Many have also demonstrated their familiarity with new words learned through the activities both in their reading of other texts and in their own writing.

CASE STUDY: BILINGUAL BIG BOOKS

Karen Johnstone of St Mary's Church of England Combined School in Slough involved a Year 6 class in producing bilingual big books for younger children in the school.

The children started out by discussing what makes an effective and enjoyable book for four to five year olds and decided on the content, characters and storyline for several picture books. They then worked in groups of four or five to make an eight grid story board.

Each group first chose their own characters and settings and made rough sketches, ensuring plenty of action for younger children to discuss before they attempted reading. They then added short, easy-to-read captions which carefully complemented the illustrations.

When the children were happy with their storyboards, they drew the full scale illustrations onto A3 pieces of paper. They wrote the captions on strips of paper which they blue-tacked to the books. Translations for the English text were supplied by parents on separate strips of paper and added to the book. Finally, the finished products – two books in Panjabi, two in Urdu and two in Hindi – were tried out with children in reception and Year 1 classes.

Each Year 6 bilingual child was matched with a younger pupil who spoke the same language. In evaluating the books, children were encouraged to think about whether their partner was:

- happy to talk about the pictures, characters and story
- able to read in their home language
- able to read the English text.

All the children responded enthusiastically, happy to discuss what was happening and to 'read' the story from the pictures.

7 Writing in other languages

Chinese version of 'Ceri'. Characters correspond to meaning not words. The only way of conveying a non-Chinese name is to find the Chinese word which corresponds most closely to each syllable. Here *Ce* is conveyed by the character at the top and *ri* by the character below

Traditionally the different language skills were considered to be in a hierarchical relationship: listening preceded speaking which in turn preceded reading and writing. More recently, these skills have been seen as inter-related, development in one area consolidating progress in the others. The division into reading and writing in this book is simply an organizational convenience: in many of the activities described, reading and writing cannot be separated.

The acquisition of writing skills in the first language is a worthy aim in itself. However, as was the case for reading, first language writing can also serve as a bridge to literacy in English. By encouraging the use of community languages in writers' workshops or dialogue journal writing, teachers are promoting children's development as writers. There are also status issues: by being allowed to use their community language, they are able to take part on equal terms in activities which would be beyond their reach in English.

Opportunities for children to write in their community languages not only help develop their literacy skills but also create a larger pool of reading resources in other languages. Professionally produced books, posters and labels can be supplemented by materials produced by children and parents. These can be handwritten or wordprocessed. When languages such as Urdu, Chinese and Japanese have a calligraphic tradition, the end result is often impressive. The same is true of wordprocessed materials – the high status attached to the new technology transfers to the end product.

Writing in other languages is also a valuable focus for language study. Children are fascinated by other scripts: they are eager to learn about the history of writing, the differences between writing systems and how writing is taught in other countries or in community language classes. They also enjoy writing simple things in other languages – especially their names. Biliterate children have a fund of knowledge which they are happy to share with their monolingual peers.

In this part of the book, we look at a range of ways in which teachers can usefully promote writing in other languages

- as a bridge to literacy in English
- as a way of encouraging children's literacy in community languages
- as a focus for language study for monolingual and bilingual children.

First language as a bridge to literacy

There is no shortage of research evidence that a sound foundation in the first language – spoken and written – creates the best conditions for the acquisition of second and subsequent languages. Literacy in the first language should therefore be promoted as an end in itself. However, it can also serve as a very valuable bridge for the acquisition of reading and writing in English.

Even if children are familiar with a different script, their knowledge of how writing works will stand them in good stead as they start to make meaning of English print. In the early days, when their knowledge of English is very limited, there will be many tasks and activities which may be beyond their grasp in English, but which can none the less be undertaken in their first language alongside their English-speaking peers.

Writers' workshops

Writers' workshops and other forms of process writing require children to look on writing as a craft involving several different stages – choosing a topic, drafting, revising, editing and finally 'publishing' their work for a wider audience. This approach is very supportive of the development of bilingual learners. It provides opportunities for children to rehearse ideas, vocabulary and structures; it also makes it clear that children are not expected to produce perfect copy at the first attempt and so helps reduce the anxiety and sense of failure associated with 'corrected' work.

While it is clearly very difficult for language learners to write in English in the early stages, there is no reason why they cannot draft, revise and edit in their first language. This approach allows them to develop their skills while joining in the same activity as their peers. It can also enhance their status in the class. Instead of emphasizing what they cannot do, the focus shifts to their achievements. This is precisely what happened with Julia, a ten year old girl who had recently arrived from Russia. Classmates – and teacher – were fascinated by the appearance of the Cyrillic script on the page and very impressed by her beautiful handwriting. A Russian-speaking member of staff provided a translation so that she was able to share her story with the class.

Julia's 'published' work produced in writers' workshop

Dialogue journals

Dialogue journals – written conversations between a child and a more experienced partner, usually the teacher or another adult – also offer opportunities for first language writing. The emphasis is on meaning, not on accuracy. The more experienced writer responds to what their partner has to say rather than to surface features. They can model appropriate grammar, vocabulary, spelling and punctuation in their replies, but they never 'correct'. Freed from the usual stresses, children are more prepared to take the risks which will help them develop as writers.

Dialogue journals have been found effective not only with native speakers, but also with children learning English. In this case, the journal can take the form of interactive picture books where the teacher labels or provides a caption for the child's picture. But it is also possible to ask a bilingual colleague or an older child to translate the journal entries for the teacher or to act as a response partner for the child in question. Children are often ready to communicate their thoughts in a journal much earlier than they are prepared to speak.

Note taking

The point of note taking is to record and remember information; the choice of language is usually irrelevant. The same is true of a number of other activities, including brainstorming, planning and discussion within a same language group, where the focus is on developing ideas rather than communicating with the wider group.

Concept keyboards

Concept keyboards can be used instead of, or in addition to, a conventional keyboard. The 128 squares which make up the keyboard can be programmed in such

A concept keyboard overlay for the Scenario program, Elmtree Farm, in Chinese produced by Hounslow Language Service

a way that when children press a word or picture on a paper overlay, a word appears on the screen. The overlays can be used to provide key words which children can then incorporate into their writing at a touch. Teachers can either program the concept keyboard themselves or buy commercial packages. Overlays for a number of programs in common usage are available in a wide range of languages. It is also possible to make your own translations with the help of bilingual colleagues or parents.

Concept keyboards are usually associated with younger children. They can, however, be used to considerable effect throughout the primary years and even with beginner bilinguals in secondary school. They are particularly useful in mixed language groups. Second language learners who are already literate touch the words in their own language, which then appear in English on the screen. Monolingual peers can model the correct English pronunciation, while bilingual learners tell them how to say the equivalent in their first language.

Community language literacy

Children who write fluently in their community languages are – inevitably – those who have attended school in the home country or invested a great deal of time and effort in community classes or at home, supported by their parents. None the less, opportunities for writing in the community language at school can be very valuable for both consolidating existing skills and making clear the importance which the school attaches to biliteracy.

Perhaps the most common reason for writing in other languages is the production of dual language materials to supplement the commercial resources available in the school. Very often these are handwritten by children or parents; increasingly, however, schools are investing in multilingual wordprocessing software.

Multilingual wordprocessing

Wordprocessing in languages which use non-Latin scripts is a relatively recent development in schools. Early initiatives suggest that multilingual wordprocessing has a very wide range of educational applications. It provides teachers with a cheap and semi-professional way of producing multilingual resources. It helps to raise the status of community languages and throws light on many new or unfamiliar aspects of language use. It also has considerable potential for more actively involving parents from other language communities.

Points to consider when introducing multilingual wordprocessing for the first time include the choice of software, the training needs of staff, parents and children and the organization of access to the computer.

Choice of software

Choice of software is narrowed down by what will run on your computer, how much you can afford and why you need the multilingual application. When deciding on a package, things to consider include:

- Character design and fonts: low resolution is sometimes a problem and can affect the readability of scripts with complex letter forms.
- Wordprocessing requirements: children need a word processor that is easy to use and allows them to play with their own and other languages. Teachers producing resources may be more interested in features such as well-drawn characters or the facility to change size and embolden.
- Accessing the other language: sometimes the arrangement follows the typewriter keyboard of the language in question, while on other occasions characters are assigned to their nearest equivalent sounds on the English keyboard.
- Special functions: programs for languages like Urdu and Arabic may offer 'contextual analysis' which automatically produces the correct character variant for any given position in the word. Programs for languages like Bengali and Gujarati may allow the user to press a special key between characters to produce a conjunct form.

Training

Teachers need time both to work alongside an experienced user of the program and to practise independently. Questions to consider when planning training include:

- Who is going to be offered training? It is a good idea to involve all bilingual colleagues in the initial sessions.
- Who is offering the training? Will teachers be able to contact the trainer easily when they meet with problems later?
- When will the training session(s) take place and how long will they last? The answers to these questions will depend on the availability of the trainer and the practicalities around releasing staff. However, it is worth considering at the outset how much opportunity there will be for hands-on experience as well as follow-up to initial training.
- How will the skills acquired be 'cascaded'? Teachers involved in the initial training will need to pass on their newly acquired skills to parents and children. (See the case study on 'Unexpected benefits of multilingual wordprocessing' below).

Access to the computer

The cost of software may mean that multilingual wordprocessing is available on only one machine. If so, careful thought needs to be given to access. Parents, for instance, may feel inhibited about coming into the classroom to practise their keyboard skills.

When the same computer is used for a range of other purposes, it may also be worth considering acquiring a separate keyboard with the other language letter forms attached. Alternative solutions, such as leaning a photocopied version of the other language arrangements against the English keyboard, are a great deal more cumbersome.

CASE STUDY: UNEXPECTED BENEFITS OF MULTILINGUAL WORDPROCESSING

Redlands Primary School in Reading boasts some 28 different languages, from Arabic to Yoruba. There is a certain irony, then, that in spite of efforts to promote the full range of languages, it is the network of French clubs run by parent volunteers in lunch time and after school which has traditionally attracted most attention from the children.

The interests of Pakistani children who form the largest linguistic minority in the school, were served by an Urdu club, attended until fairly recently by half a dozen faithful and enthusiastic girls – a rather striking contrast with the much larger number of francophiles.

When multilingual wordprocessing was introduced at Redlands, staff and children had already identified a wide range of possible uses, including dual language books, Urdu and English versions of the same book, labels for displays and letters home. However, no one anticipated even more impressive benefits unrelated to the printed word.

The impact on children has been dramatic, kick-started by a description of Urdu club activities in a school assembly at the beginning of the year and helped along by a large display in the Infant Hall of wordprocessed names and simple sentences in Urdu. Peer tutoring has proved a prominent feature, with more experienced children providing scaffolding for novices.

Parents have also played a crucial role in moving the project forward. The wordprocessor was launched by the two Urdu-speaking teachers at a termly informal gathering attended by many women from the Asian community. It was suspected that levels of literacy in Urdu were low and great care was taken to present the project without intimidating the women.

This sensitivity appears to have been misplaced. Pakistani mothers previously reluctant to have anything to do with computers showed great excitement at seeing the word 'Welcome' written in Urdu on the screen. By the end of the session, everyone had keyed in and printed their names in Nastaliq script.

The women's own accounts left no doubt as to their fascination: 'It was so amazing. I was telling my husband about it when I got home – I told him I was typing on an English computer and watching Urdu coming up on the screen!'

A follow-up workshop built on this initial enthusiasm. Parents drafted stories on paper, working mostly in pairs and seeking feedback from their peers and the Urdu-speaking teachers. Later they began keying their stories, using the computer as a typewriter rather than an aid to composition. This seemed the most prudent course to follow for parents with little experience of the new technology. At the end of the session, several of the women voiced their interest in coming into school on a regular basis to practise their newly acquired skills.

Teachers already feeling hard-pressed by other demands found it difficult at first to see how extra time could be found for helping parents. Parents were sensitive to this problem and willing to negotiate support and structure for their own learning. In fact, the way forward was suggested by a mother concerned not to make unreasonable demands on teacher time: 'Once you've learnt to set it up and got started, you can get on and learn by yourself.' Or, as another mother commented, 'It'll be more useful and more used if we can learn to use it.'

In practice, a kind of cascade training has evolved. Time initially invested by a member of staff in working with one particularly enthusiastic mother has reaped ample rewards as she, in turn, has been able to help other parents and children.

Another very practical step has been to move the computer to the Infant Hall at lunchtimes. Mothers had felt inhibited about working in the classroom, where they were distracted by what was going on around them and worried that they, for their part, were distracting the children.

The outputs of multilingual wordprocessing anticipated at the outset have been achieved: dual language books, communications home in Urdu, teaching materials for the Urdu club. The other benefits, though, are even more impressive. In a number of cases, women whose English is limited and who have not felt able to take a part in school-related activities have made a contribution to children's school learning for the first time.

Redlands prides itself on being a welcoming school with high levels of community involvement but, up to the present, relatively few Pakistani families have taken an active role. Staff are excited by recent developments. They have been surprised to find how many mothers are literate in Urdu and how quickly they overcame their initial computer phobia.

Pakistani children have openly expressed pleasure at the expert help provided by their mothers. They have also grown in confidence around computers and also in their writing skills in Urdu, and are clearly enjoying their newly acquired expert status. English children, for their part, are showing an unprecedented level of interest in learning to speak, read and write in Urdu.

Writing and language study

The history of writing is a very productive area for language study for children of all ages. The presence of children who are familiar with writing systems from all over the world adds an extra dimension of interest to class explorations of this subject. The extent of human ingenuity is evident from the range of different solutions that have been devised for recording speech in writing.

Different scripts

Alphabetic writing systems use letters – or combinations of letters – to represent both vowels and consonants. Some languages use a roman alphabet adapted to their own particular sound system. But there are also other alphabets, including the Greek, and the Cyrillic which is used for languages such as Russian and Serbian. The Korean alphabet is particularly interesting: when vowels are added to consonants, they are sometimes placed at the side and in other cases above, depending on the visual effect.

Many Indian languages use a rather different system in which letters represent syllables. The scripts for languages such as Bengali, Gujarati and Hindi hang down from the line rather than resting on it as in English.

Another system found widely in the Indian sub-continent is the consonantal writing used for Urdu. Here, as in Arabic, the focus is on consonants – vowels are marked optionally with diacritic marks above or below the letters. Another feature is the range of variants: the shape of most letters changes according to

whether they are initial, medial, final or appear in isolation. A third important difference is that Urdu and Arabic writing runs from right to left. Hebrew also uses consonantal writing and runs from right to left.

Chinese writing is, of course, based on entirely different principles and focuses on meaning rather than sound. The varieties spoken in different parts of China can be as different as Spanish and Italian, or German and Dutch. Yet they are all written with the same characters or logographs. A good parallel can be found in the use of number symbols in a very wide range of languages. The number 5, for instance, is *cinq* in French, *pump* in Welsh, *cinco* in Spanish and *five* in English. Chinese characters are written in a notional square, each stroke added in a given sequence. Traditionally the characters range from top to bottom and right to left, though increasingly Chinese is written horizontally from left to right.

Probably the most complex system of all is the mixed writing system used for Japanese. It consists of a combination of kanji or Chinese characters and two quite different syllabic writing systems, hiragana and katakana. The main content words are often written in kanji, additional grammatical information is given in hiragana and katakana is used extensively for representing English or any foreign words other than those of Chinese origin.

Further reading

- *Handbook of scripts and alphabets* by George Campbell (Routledge, 1997).

Handwriting practice in Russian

Handwriting practice in Chinese

Learning to write

Approaches to the teaching of writing vary enormously, even within languages which use the same writing system. Chinese children learn to write on squared paper; American children use guide lines for the formation of lower and upper case letters; Russian copy books have a diagonal line to guide the slope of the letter.

Many children learn to write at home or in community classes. They are usually very happy to bring in the primers and copy books they are using and to demonstrate how they set about the task of writing. Their monolingual peers are often equally eager to learn about another writing system and are especially interested in finding out how to write their own names.

Awareness of scripts

Awareness of different writing systems develops very quickly. Most bilingual pre-school children are able to distinguish between different scripts at about the same time as they learn to differentiate numbers and letters.

Other scripts are in fact all around us – on food wrappers, instruction manuals and shop signs. Children can be encouraged to bring in examples of other scripts from home. Bilingual children will, of course, have access to a wide range of printed material, from calendars to newspapers. Samples of other scripts can be incorporated into displays. They can also be used for fun activities such as 'Spot the script' (see opposite).

How many scripts do you recognise?

فَسَقَطَ عَـلَى الأَرْضِ بِعُنْفٍ ،سَيَحْتَاجُ

Hổ giật mình quay lại, đã thấy Cóc

Την επόμενη μέρα στο σχολείο

সাফিনের সাথে খেলতে তার কেমন

پھر عمران کو ایک مشکل پیش آئی ۔ وہ بولا میری مدد کرو !

પરંતુ હિપોપૉટેમસની એક વાત ચિત્તાને હેરાન કરતી

ਮੇਰੇ ਮਾਤਾ ਜੀ ਨਾਸ਼ਤਾ ਲਿਆ ਰਹੇ ਹਨ ।

出門時 ， 蓋爾穿上短上衣。

и кров сав од пламена

தமிழ் ஒரு மொழி. தனித் தமிழ் ஒரு

salamadhlaha u qurux badnaan lahaa!

Languages from top to bottom:
Arabic
Vietnamese
Greek
Bengali
Urdu (Nastaliq)
Gujarati
Panjabi (Gurmukhi)
Chinese
Russian
Tamil
Somali

Spot the script

CASE STUDY: NAMEPLATES IN NASTALIQ

Interesting work on Islamic calligraphy and design grew spontaneously from a project on writing and communication with Year 6 children at Redlands Primary School in Reading.

The class teacher, Elizabeth Pye, had linked the history of different writing systems with different holy books. Children compared different versions of the Bible and brought in copies of the Qu'rān from home. They had also experimented with a range of different writing tools and materials, including Chinese brushes and ink blocks.

As part of the project, children had been asked to design name-plates using templates with a repeating eight point star shape as a border. Islamic patterns were part of the cultural tradition of Pakistani and other Muslim children, but every member of the class had been exposed to Islamic art through looking at pic-tures of tiles and mosques; they also had experience of colouring Islamic patterns as part of their exploration of shape and space in maths.

By chance, Asya, a sixteen year old Pakistani girl and former pupil, arrived for a week's work experience at the school when the class was working on the project. One of the children asked Asya to write their name in Nastaliq script as the centrepoint of their design. Asya duly pencilled in the name for them to trace over and was soon responding to other requests for help. The exercise generated a great deal of discussion and interest in calligra-phy. Alice, for instance, said she liked the style of writing: 'It was a new experience. It was fancy and decorative and I liked the way it flowed.' The end products were certainly impressive.

 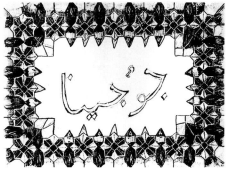

Name-plates in Nastaliq script produced by Year 6 children

8 Endnote

Several themes run through this book which challenge the biblical notion of Babel as a place of chaos.

Diversity as a resource

Perhaps the most important of these themes is that diversity is a resource and not a problem. For a considerable period of time, bilingualism was pathologized: the emphasis was on the negative – the fact that children have limited proficiency in English – rather on the positive – the fact that they are highly competent speakers of a least one other language. Monolingual myopia detracted attention from the fact that in most parts of the world multilingualism is the norm. Yet the ability to speak more than one language is undoubtedly an asset, not an obstacle to progress. Bilingualism has increased the vision and broadened the audience of politicians like Pierre Trudeau and literary giants like Rabindranath Tagore; it offers similar advantages to children from the diverse communities served by schools throughout the English-speaking world.

Monolingual teachers and children can only benefit from contact with bilingual colleagues and peers. The presence of individuals whose experience spans different languages and cultures reminds us that there are many different ways of seeing and responding to the world, a very important lesson for life. Multilingual classrooms provide an ideal setting for challenging stereotypes and for encouraging cooperation and empathy for other points of view.

Opportunities for language study are also transformed in classrooms where bilingual children are encouraged to share their experience of life in two languages. For example, bilingual students at Lanfranc High School taught their classmates simple conversational routines in a variety of languages. This project clearly had far-reaching implications for the participants: one boy who had initially been very resistant was clearly won over and had nothing but praise for his fellow student and 'teacher', Bashir. Children at Godolphin Junior School learned to answer the register and exchange greetings in Urdu, Panjabi, French and German. At Redlands Primary School, English-speaking children now have a clearer understanding of how writing works – from right to left as well as left to right – as a result of work with an Urdu-speaking visitor. These are just some of the examples included in *The power of Babel* which demonstrate how monolingual children have benefited – cognitively and affectively – from the presence of bilinguals.

Activating prior knowledge

Another theme which runs through this book is the way in which children's progress in English is accelerated – and not impeded – when attention is paid to the other languages they speak. All too often, children are treated as though no learning takes place outside their English language schooling. Yet when teachers take steps to activate prior knowledge, the classroom can seem a far more comprehensible place, in which children can take more responsibility for their learning. This was the case, for instance, for Bangladeshi boys in an East London comprehensive school who took part in an experiment in paired reading.

Those more experienced in English supported the reading of more recent arrivals in a variety of ways, including the use of Bengali to explain the meaning of key words in English; recent arrivals were able to reciprocate by supporting peers schooled in the UK in reading Bengali texts.

A developmental sequence?

The case studies included in this book are based on the experience of teachers attending courses on 'Meeting the needs of multilingual pupils'. In some cases, the majority of children in their schools were bilingual; in others, most children spoke English only. In some cases, there was one predominant language in addition to English; in others, many different languages were represented. The teachers were offered suggestions for a variety of school based projects spanning English language and bilingual support.

The fact that most teachers chose to start with projects to promote linguistic diversity came as a surprise since, in our experience, teachers are usually more anxious to acquire specific English language teaching skills. However, the reactions of almost 200 course participants point to the developmental sequence mirrored in the structure of this book. First teachers need to build up a clear picture of the nature and extent of diversity; then they need to explore ways of responding to diversity in the curriculum and organization of their schools. The focus on second language teaching issues comes after – and not before – the school has considered wider issues of cultural and linguistic diversity.

Whole school development

One final note of caution should be sounded. The teachers who provided case study material reported both personal growth and changes in practice from which all the children in their charge benefited. In some cases, a number of other colleagues were involved directly or indirectly in their projects; in others, teachers expressed frustration because the attitudes of headteachers made it difficult for them to move forward. The experience of the initiatives discussed in this book, and many others, is that senior managers and whole school policy are essential for any meaningful change.

9 Useful names and addresses

Organizations

Access to Information on Multicultural Education Resources (AIMER)

Reading and Language Information Centre
The University of Reading
Bulmershe Court
Reading RG6 1HY

tel: +44 (0)118 931 8820
fax: +44 (0)118 931 6801

email: ehsabbas@reading.ac.uk

website: http://www.rdg.ac.uk/AcaDepts/eh/
ReadLang/aimer.htm

AIMER is a database project which offers information on multicultural, anti-racist teaching materials. It publishes the *AIMER Yearbook: photocopiable resources to support the multicultural dimension of the national curriculum*, as well as individual resources lists which make up the Yearbook.

Association of Teachers of English to Speakers of Other Languages (ATESOL)

Joint Council Building
Leichhardt Primary School
Corner Marion & Norton Sts
Leichhardt 2040
Australia

tel: +61 29 564 3322

Centre for Information of Language Teaching and Research (CILT)

20 Bedfordbury
London WC2N 4LB

tel: +44 (0)171 379 5101

fax: +44 (0)171 379 5082

email: library@ cilt.org.uk

Information on all aspects of language teaching. Produces the CILT *Community Languages Bulletin*.

National Association for Language Development in the Curriculum (NALDIC)

South West Herts LCSC
Holywell School Site
Tolpits Lane
Watford WD1 8NT

tel: +44 (0)1923 248584
fax: +44 (0)1923 225130

NALDIC is a professional body for all those interested in raising the achievement of pupils with English as an additional language. It aims to disseminate information on current developments in curriculum and language teaching, drawing on the thinking and practice of colleagues working with pupils of all ages, both nationally and internationally. It also aims to represent the views of teachers and other professional workers on educational issues which affect the teaching and learning of bilingual pupils.

Primary English Teaching Association (PETA)

Laura Street
New Town 2042
Australia

tel: +61 2 565 1277
fax: +61 2 565 1070

email: primeng@peg.apc.org

PETA is committed to serving as a professional forum for the sharing of developments, ideas and philosophies relevant to the of spoken and written language in the teaching and learning of English.

Reading and Language Information Centre (RALIC)

The University of Reading
Bulmershe Court
Reading RG6 1HY

tel: +44 (0)118 931 8820
fax: +44 (0)118 931 6801

email: reading-centre @reading.ac.uk

website: http://www.rdg.ac.uk/AcaDepts/eh/ReadLanghome.html

Engaged in research on language and literacy and offers a range of courses and conferences around language and literacy. Unique resources collection of 14,000 children's books and audiovisual materials. Specialist interest in multilingual classrooms.

Teachers of English To Speakers of Other Languages Inc (TESOL)

1600 Cameron Street
Suite 300
Alexandria
Va. 22314–2751

tel: +1 703 836–0774
fax: +1 703 836–7864

website: http://www.ncbe.gwu.edu/tesol/abouttes.html

An association for teachers who teach English as a second or foreign language, students, and publishers whose aims are improving the teaching of English as a second or foreign language by promoting research, disseminating information, developing guidelines and promoting certification.

TESL Association of Ontario

27 Carlton Street
Suite 405
Toronto
Ontario M5B 1L2

tel: (+1) 416 593–4234

email: teslon@inforamp.net

This organization aims to advance effective instruction, to determine needs in the field and to work to enhance the learning environment in the area of English as a Second Language (ESL) and English Skills Development (ESD) in Ontario. It also aims to provide opportunities for professional development, to establish and ensure standards in teaching, and to advise all agencies responsible for the administration of ESL/ESD.

TESL Canada Federation

PO Box 44105
Burnaby
British Columbia V5B 4Y2

tel/fax: +1 604 298–0312 or 1–800–393–9199

email: admin@tesl.ca

website: http://www.tesl.ca

TESL Canada is a national organization ded-
icated to advancing communication and
coordinating awareness of issues for those
concerned with English as a second language and English skills development. The
organization promotes advocacy for ESL
learners, unifies teachers and learners by
providing a forum and network capabili-
ties, supports the sharing of knowledge and
experiences across Canada, and represents
diverse needs and interests in TESL nationally and internationally.

Publishers and book distributors

Barnet Education Support and Training

Media Resources Officer
Inspection and Advicory Service
Barnet Professional Development Centre
451 High Road
Finchley
London N12 0AS

tel: +44 (0)181 359 2000

Produces learning materials including a
range of multilingual notices for schools in
Chinese, English, Farsi, Greek, Gujarati and
Urdu with 'add-on' strips in Arabic, Bengali,
Hebrew, Hindi, Japanese, Panjabi, Somali
and Turkish.

Bedfordshire Multicultural Resource Centre

c/o Section 11 Project
Leagrove Junior School
Strangers Way
Luton LU4 9ND

Distributor of *Learning to learn in a second language* by Pauline Gibbons.

Child's Play International Ltd

Ashworth Road
Bridgemead
Swindon SN5 7YD

tel: +44 (0)1793 616286

Produces several titles in half a dozen European languages.

Collins Educational

77–85 Fulham Palace Road
Hammersmith
London W6 8JB

tel: +44 (0)181 741 7070
export: +44 (0)141 306 3391

Produces 'Welcome' poster in many
languages.

ComStar Company

20432 Silverado Avenue
Suite 212
Cupertino, CA 95014
email: info@gy.com
tel: (+1) 408–257–9480
fax: (+1) 408–446–5359.
website: http://www.gy.com

Produces a digest of multilingual software, books, CDs, cassettes and videos for over 150 different languages.

Hounslow Language Service

Hounslow Education Centre
Martindale Road
Hounclow TW4 7HE
tel: +44 (0)181 570 4186

Produces a range of learning materials including multilingual concept keyboard overlays for Scenario and Podd programs.

Learning Media Ltd

Level 3
State Services Commission Building
100 Moelsworth Street
Box 3293
Wellington
New Zealand.
tel: +64 (0)4 471 6064
fax: +64 (0)4 472 6444

Producers of a range of books in Maori and other Pacific languages for the New Zealand government.

Magi Publications

112 Whitfield Street
London W1P 5RU
tel: +44 (0)171 387 0610

Publishes dual language books in a range of languages.

Mantra Publishing

5 Alexandra Grove
London N12 8NU
tel: +44 (0)181 445 5123

Publishes dual language books and audio-cassettes in a range of languages.

Multilingual Books and Tapes

4748 University Way
Seattle, WA 98105
tel: (+1) 206 522 2488
fax: (+1) 206 522 1050
Orders: (+1) 1 800 218 2737
email: esl@esl.net
website: http://www.esl.net.mbt

Supplier of materials in over 100 languages in book, audio, video or computer formats.

Partnership Publishing

Bradford & Ilkley Community College
Department of Teaching Studies
Bradford
West Yorkshire BD7 1AY

Publishes a small number of dual language books in Urdu and English using highly innovative designs.

Primary English Teaching Association (PETA)

see Organizations above

Publishes books and other practical materials especially written with the needs of teachers in mind.

Reading and Language Information Centre (RALIC)

see Organizations above

Specializes in practical publications for teachers, including several titles of specific interest to teachers in multilingual classrooms.

Roy Yates Books

Smallfields Cottage
Cox Green

Rudgwick
Horsham
West Sussex RH12 3DE

tel: +44 (0)1403 822299

Lists and supplies every known dual language book in the UK and other English-speaking countries, along with many other multilingual resources from all over the world.

SRA McGraw Hill

Shoppenhangers Road
Maidenhead SL6 2QL

tel: +44 (0)1628 23432

Suppliers of the *Stick-on storybooks: wordless books to write and read* series

Tower Hamlets Language Support Service

Professional Development Centre
English Street
Mile End
London E3 4TA

tel: +44 (0)171 364 6383

Publishes a range of English languages support materials.

Bilingual theatre

Half Moon Young People's Theatre

New Half Moon Theatre,
43 White Horse Road,
London E1 0ND

tel: +44 (0)171 265 8138.

M6 Theatre Company

Hamer County Primary School,
Albert Royds Street,
Rochdale OL16 2SU

tel: +44 (0)1706 355898

10 References and further reading

Alladina, S. (1995) *Being bilingual: a guide for parents, teachers and young people on mother tongue, heritage language and bilingual education*. Stoke-on-Trent: Trentham Books.

Baetens-Beardsmore, H. (1994) *European models of bilingual education*. Clevedon, Philadelphia & Adelaide: Multilingual Matters.

Bailey, K. & Savage, L. (eds) (1994) *New ways in teaching speaking*. Alexandria, Virginia: TESOL

Baker, C. (1995) *A parents' and teachers' guide to bilingualism*. Clevedon, Philadelphia & Adelaide: Multilingual Matters.

Baker, C. (1996) *Foundations of bilingual education and bilingualism*. Clevedon, Philadelphia & Adelaide: Multilingual Matters.

Baker, C. & Price, S. (1998) *The encyclopedia of bilingualism and bilingual education*. Clevedon: Multilingual Matters

Baynham, M. (1995) *Literacy practices*. Harlow: Longman.

Beykont, Z. (1994) Academic progress of a non-dominant group: a longitudinal study of Puerto Ricans in New York City's late exit bilingual programs. Unpublished doctoral dissertation. Harvard University Graduate School of Education.

Campbell, G. (1997) *Concise compendium of the world's languages*. London: Routledge.

Campbell, G. (1997) *Handbook of scripts and alphabets*. London: Routledge.

Campos, J. & Keatinge, R. (1988) The Capinteria language minority student experience: from theory, to practice, to success. In T. Skutnabb-Kangas & J. Cummins (eds), *Minority education: from shame to struggle*. Clevedon, Philadelphia & Adelaide: Multilingual Matters, pp. 299–308.

Coelho, E. (1988) *Caribbean students in Canadian schools*. Toronto: Carib-Can publishers.

Coelho, E. (1998) *Teaching and learning in multicultural classrooms*. Clevedon, Philadelphia & Adelaide: Multilingual Matters.

Comrie, B., Matthews, S. & Polensky, M. (1996) *The atlas of world languages*. London: Bloomsbury.

Cummins, J. (1984) *Bilingualism and special education: issues in assessment and pedagogy*. Clevedon, Philadelphia & Adelaide: Multilingual Matters.

Cummins, J. (1996) *Negotiating identities: education for empowerment in a diverse society*. Ontario, Ca: California Association for Bilingual Education and Stoke-on-Trent: Trentham Books.

Dalphinis, M. (1991) The Afro-English creole speech community. In S. Alladina & V. Edwards (eds) *Multilingualism in the British Isles*, volume 2. London: Longman.

Day, R. (ed.) (1993) *New ways in teaching reading*. Alexandria, Virginia: TESOL.

Department for Education & Welsh Office (1995) *English in the national curriculum*. London: HMSO.

Edwards, V. (1986) *Language in a Black community*. Clevedon, Philadelphia & Adelaide: Multilingual Matters.

Edwards, V. (1991) The Welsh speech community. In S. Alladina & V. Edwards (eds) *Multilingualism in the British Isles*, volume 1. London: Longman, pp. 107–25.

Edwards, V. (1995) *Reading in multilingual classrooms*. Reading: Reading and Language Information Centre

Edwards, V. (1995) *Speaking in multilingual classrooms*. Reading: Reading and Language Information Centre

Edwards, V. (1995) *Writing in multilingual classrooms*. Reading: Reading and Language Information Centre

Edwards, V. (1996) *The other languages: a guide to multilingual classrooms*. Reading: Reading and Language Information Centre. Revised and extended Australian version, Newtown, NSW: Primary English Teaching Association, 1997.

Gibbons, P. (1991) *Learning to learn in a second language*. Newtown, Australia: Primary English Teaching Association.

Gillborn, D. & Gipps, C. (1996) *Recent research on the achievements of ethnic minority pupils*. London: OFSTED.

Grange Road first School (1993) *Send for Sohail!* Bradford: Partnership Teaching.

Gregory, E. (1993) *Sweet and sour: learning to read in a British and Chinese school*. English in Education 27(3): 53–9.

Gregory, E. (1996) *Making sense of a new world: learning to read in a second language*. London: Paul Chapman.

Gregory, E. (1998) Siblings as mediators of literacy in linguistic minority communities. *Language and Education* 12(1).

Hall, D. (1995) *Assessing the needs of bilingual pupils: living in two languages. London*: David Fulton.

Hazareesingh, S. with Kenway, P. & Simms, K. (1994) *Speaking about the past: oral history for 5–7 year olds*. Stoke-on-Trent: Trentham Books.

Heath, S.B. (1983) *Ways with words: language and life in communities and classrooms*. Cambridge: Cambridge University Press.

Jabeen, Z. (1992) *The moving mango tree and other tales*. Bradford: Partnership Teaching.

Jones, M. (1996) *The balloon detectives*. Bradford: Partnership Teaching

Katzner, K. (1994) *Languages of the world*. London: Routledge.

Keel, P (ed.) (1994) *Assessment in the multi-ethnic primary classroom*. Stoke-on-Trent: Trentham Books.

Lamey, J. (1989) The power of partners. *The English Magazine* 22: 24–8.

Lucas, T. & Katz, A. (1994) Reframing the debate: the roles of native languages in English-only programs for language minority students. *TESOL Quarterly* 28(3): 537–62.

MacKinnon, K. (1991) The Gaelic speech community. In S. Alladina & V. Edwards (eds.) *Multilingualism in the British Isles*, volume 1. London: Longman, pp. 49–67.

Marenbon, J. (1987) *English, our English: the new orthodoxy examined*. London: Centre for Policy Studies.

Multilingual Resources for Children Project (1995) *Building bridges: multilingual resources for children*. Clevedon, Philadelphia & Adelaide: Multingual Matters.

National Center for Educational Statistics (1994) *Mini-digest of educational statistics 1994*. Washington DC: US Department of Education.

Nicholas, J. (1994) *Language diversity surveys as agents of change*. Clevedon, Philadelphia & Adelaide: Multilingual Matters.

Ogbu, J. (1992) Understanding cultural diversity and learning. *Educational Researcher* 21(8): 5–14 & 24.

Passmore, B. (1994) Section 11 is back into the melting pot. *Times Education Supplement* March 10:25

Ramirez, J. (1992) Executive summary. *Bilingual Research Journal* 16: 1–62.

Rutter, J. (1994) *Refugee children in the classroom*. Stoke-on-Trent: Trentham Books.

Rutter, J. & Jones, C. (1997) *Mapping the field: new initiatives in refugee education*. Stoke-on-Trent: Trentham Books.

Taylor, W. & Piché, D. (1991) *A report on short changing children: the impact of fiscal inequality on the education of students at risk*. Washington DC: US House of Representatives, Committee on Education and Labor.

Thomas, W. & Collier, V. (1997) *School effectiveness and language minority students*. Washington DC: National Clearinghouse for Bilingual Education.

Verhoeven, L. (1994) Acquisition of biliteracy. *AILA Review* 8: 61–74.

Walker, S., Edwards, V. & Leonard, H. (1998) *Write around the world*. Reading: Reading and Language Information Centre

Wong Fillmore, L. (1991) When learning a second language means losing the first. *Early Childhood Research Quarterly* 6: 323–46.

Index